THE PEREGRINE
FALCON

THE PEREGRINE FALCON

BY ROBERT MURPHY

ILLUSTRATED BY TECO SLAGBOOM

HOUGHTON MIFFLIN COMPANY BOSTON

Library of Congress Cataloging in Publication Data
Murphy, Robert William, date
  The peregrine falcon.
  1. Peregrine falcon—Legends and stories.
I. Title.
[PS3563.U75P4   1981]   813'.54   80-26873
ISBN 0-395-30860-7 (pbk.)

Printed in the United States of America

M 10 9 8 7 6 5 4 3 2 1

Houghton Mifflin Company paperback 1981

FOR MY MOTHER

There's night and day, brother,
both sweet things; sun, moon, and
stars, brother, all sweet things; there's
likewise a wind on the heath. Life is
very sweet, brother; who would wish
to die?

GEORGE BORROW
Lavengro

CONTENTS

PART I

THE BARRENS

THE INUKOK

THE ROCKY NARROWS of Chesterfield Inlet and the long, bleak, downlike hills of the Barren Grounds, dun-colored and patched with the melting snow of spring, lay beneath the falcon as he circled on an updraft from the warming earth. The rising column of air pressed buoyantly upward beneath him, against his spread tail and long narrow wings, and as he circled ever higher in it, finding its limits and staying within them, the horizons of the great silent land moved out. The silvery thread of the frozen Inlet faded off into the mist of the southeast, where it finally emptied into Hudson Bay, and in the opposite direction he could see the pale, flat widening of the Inlet where Baker Lake flowed into it.

Below him, in the reindeer moss and under the stunted willows that branched out and spread low to the ground under the constant harassment of the wind, the warmth of the sun was hurrying the low plants of the tundra back to their short summer life. They had to bloom quickly and bear their fruit before the snow covered them again, and the earliest of them, the saxifrage with its deep pink flowers, was already starring the moss with blossoms that came up at the edge of the snow. The ground squirrels emerged from hibernation and the collared lemmings that had moved about through their dark tunnels under the snow all winter crept out blinking into the sun and sat as if hypnotized in the warmth of it. The songs of snow buntings and pipits, longspurs and wheatears, came down the wind, for the birds were arriving daily on their long migrations from the south. They were already beginning their courtships; the summer nights, so short in this latitude, would give them almost continuous daylight in which to gather food for their young and get them on the wing.

The tiercel (which is what falconers call the male peregrine, because it is a third smaller than the female) saw the comings and goings of a large number of birds from his commanding height, but ignored them. He had fed early in the morning and wasn't hungry, and the excitement of spring was building up in him to a point where he spent more time scanning the wide sky than he did hunting. He had arrived a few days ago from the Florida Keys, coming unerringly back to the cliff on the Inlet where he had established an eyrie and mated and helped his falcon raise their young the year before; and now that he was here, and had walked with his humpbacked shuffle around the ledge where the nest had been, he was restless to be alone.

For a while he soared, mounting higher and higher into the clear air, until a raven came flying up the Inlet a few feet above the rocky escarpment. The tiercel watched him, changing his circle to keep him in view; as the big black bird neared the ledge the tiercel swung a wider circle, rolled over in the air, headed down, took six or seven swift wing-beats to give himself speed, and folded his wings. He fell like a meteor; the air roared past him with a sound like ripping canvas and the raven, belatedly seeing him, croaked in fright, dropped quickly down the face of the cliff to within a foot of the ice and put on speed.

If there had been eggs or young on the ledge the tiercel would have had more deadly intentions, but now he was satisfied merely to drive the interloper away. He pulled out of his stoop, opening his wings and spreading his tail against the roaring air, turned upward and bounded high with the force of his dive until his momentum was gone. He hung for a moment, did a wingover, and dropped to a pile of stones on the top of the cliff above the ledge. This was his lookout post. From a distance it resembled a man, and was supposed to, for some Eskimo had built it purposely so that he or other Eskimos could see it as they moved in their boats along the lonely Inlet and feel less alone in the empty land. It was called *Inukok*, "manlike," and there were many of them along the Inlet's skyline. This one had flat, bright orange lichen, Caloplaca, growing down the side;

the tiercel's droppings had given the lichen a foothold on the stones and nourished it.

On top of his lookout, the tiercel puffed up his feathers and sat quietly for a while. Snow buntings sang around him and a flight of oldsquaw ducks looking for a tundra pond to pitch into passed far to the west of him. He watched them for a long moment incuriously; most of his attention was on the sky. Even in his quietness, sitting relaxed and with his breast feathers loose, he gave an impression of spirit, compactness, strong bone, and hard-muscled power: a rapier quiet in the scabbard. The feathers on his slate-blue back were as tightly laid and seemed as impervious as a coat of mail, and the wings which gave him enough speed to catch any bird on the continent were so long that the tips of their dark primaries crossed nearly at the end of his white tipped tail. There was other color on him; his breast was pale gray striped laterally with fine black lines except over his crop, which was soft salmon pink, the cere at the base of his beak and the long, taloned feet were butter-yellow with good feeding; his head was almost black, as was the distinguishing moustache mark (shared with some other falcons) that curved down from his big dark-brown eyes. His hooked upper mandible had a notch called a tooth in it, to fit between the neck vertebra of the birds he caught, for it was his habit to sever their spinal cords with a bite and kill them quickly.

He was the hunter that men had caught and trained to catch ducks and other birds for them long before gunpowder was used or thought of: for that and for his great style and spectacular powers of flight, which as groundlings bound to the earth they could watch with a lift of the heart.

For several hours the tiercel sat like a carving, only moving his head a little from side to side occasionally to keep the entire horizon in view; for although with the set of his eyes he could see most of it, there was a narrow segment behind him which he could not. His vision was far beyond that of men; he had eight times their accommodation, which showed him the single beat of a wing miles away anywhere within his view, for he didn't have man's comparatively narrow tunnel of sight but focused all over the retina.

Finally his long immobility was suddenly broken. He turned on the stone to face southeast, fixed in that direction, and began to bob his head; excitement took hold of him. He saw the falcon now; she was far off, flying a straight line high in the air, and headed to pass not far from him. *Kak! Kak!* He gave two sharp, hoarse croaks and bowed until the point of his beak nearly touched the stone, croaked several more times, straightened up, and launched into the air. He flew a short course back and forth above the escarpment. The falcon shifted her course a little and increased her wingbeats; in a surprisingly short time she was nearly over him. He dropped below the escarpment and began to make a wailing cry. *Wichew! Wichew!* He flew about, still calling, touching one enticing nesting ledge after another, showing her that the choice was wide, while she circled and looked down at him.

He increased his efforts to lure her down, still wailing. He paused for a short space on each ledge now, shuffling around on it, and then flew to the next to do the same thing as his excitement increased. The falcon broke her circle, seemed to start for the northeast again, and then returned; she was tempted. Finally she decided; she dropped with her wings half closed along her body so that the primaries pointed straight behind her, dropped her feet, rocked down through the whistling air and landed on the lookout stones with a flourish of long wings. Her long journey was over.

The tiercel flew up and landed on a high gray rock nearby, croaking and bowing in welcome. The falcon, a large bird so dark as to be almost black, gave herself a shake to settle her feathers and watched him. Now that she had decided to join him she would be rather passive in the courtship; he would be the active one, taking each of the steps which made up the ancient pattern that would be complete with their mating.

Presently, calm now and content to see her there, he grew quiet. In the cool sunlight, with the wide dun Barrens patched with snow around them, with the bird songs and the flicker of wings and the faint stirrings in the moss of lemmings and voles, they stood low on their stones and grew accustomed to one another and to being there together. They looked calmly about and preened their feathers.

After a while the tiercel stretched his wings over his back, moved to the edge of his stone, and took to the air. The smaller birds in his vicinity immediately recognized the difference in his movements and intentions. Their songs ceased and they dropped to the moss and became very still. The tiercel rose into the air, the rhythm of his wingbeats increased, and after beating for a distance down the Inlet he left it, mounted higher into the air, and moved out over the Barrens. The falcon stayed still, watching him until he was out of her sight. In half an hour or so she began to bob her head. The tiercel came into view, high in the air and with something in his foot, and his thin wailing came down the wind. *Wichew! Wichew!* The falcon wailed in reply and launched herself off the Inukok. She flew, wailing, toward him, and when he was high above her he dropped the bird that he had caught. It fell, turning with loose wings through the air. The falcon rose to meet it, and as it dropped past her she rolled sideways and caught it in one foot. The wailing stopped; they both returned to their stones and, as the tiercel watched, the falcon, holding the quarry on the stone with one foot, began to plume it. The plucked feathers drifted down the wind, and she began to eat. The compact had been sealed.

THE EYRIE

IN THE first cold pink glow of sunrise a flock of snow geese, which had been flying all night, crossed the Inlet to the east not far from the two peregrines. They were big white birds with black wingtips; the dawnlight turned them faintly rosy, and their resonant, nasal *houck! houck!* rose and fell as they talked to one another. They were looking for a place to rest and feed; they had wintered on the Gulf coast, and were going farther north to nest.

The peregrines watched them from their stones until

they were gone, shook their feathers into place, and turned their attention to the first business of the day. They were hungry. They watched the Inlet below them for a while and saw little that interested them, and presently the tiercel took off into the wind and flew out over the tundra. There were many lakes below him, for the water from the melting snow ran into the low places and lay above the impermeable permafrost until it evaporated later in the year, for there was little rainfall on the Barrens. The cycle of freezing and thawing threw up regular polygons in places between these ponds, so that parts of the land he flew over had the checkerboard appearance of cultivated land, broken here and there with rocks thrust up by the action of the frost and domes of ice. But there was no cultivation nor any human life in it; it was a soggy, blasted place and seemed in its immense sweep and desolation to be empty of life.

From his high vantage, however, the tiercel saw many creatures: arctic hares in their white coats, a few willow ptarmigan already losing their white plumage feather by feather and replacing it with brown for camouflage against the moss; birds from the south, and far off a snowy owl on his lookout of a high, rectangular stone. While the tiercel watched, the owl launched himself, swooped upon an incautious hare, and struggled with it on the ground. At some other time the tiercel might have stooped at the owl and bedeviled it for sport, but this time he swung away from it; he wanted to catch something and return to the cliff again. His hunting wasn't successful; birds of a size he might have caught and taken back to the cliff were wary of him and stayed quietly near the shores of the ponds or crouched on the tundra and he returned, several thousand feet up, with an empty foot.

The pattern of the courtship procedure was already established in him and the majority of his display was to be in his powers of flight, as that of other birds is in a display of bright plumage or an arrangement of objects or a dance. He rolled over and stooped, taking fifteen rapid wingbeats to pick up speed. He plunged two thousand feet in less than fifteen seconds, dropped into the gorge near the falcon, bounded up and into a vertical figure eight at terrific speed before her, rolled out of it at the bottom and landed on his stone.

They sat for a while, preening their feathers and occasionally wailing at one another. Presently an early phalarope from the coast of Peru flew up the Inlet. When it was opposite them they both launched into the air. The phalarope realized too late that they were after it; it put on its best speed and tried to evade them. They converged upon it, the falcon picked up her wingbeat, swung in, snatched it out of the air and returned to the Inukok with it. The tiercel went on down the Inlet, caught a longspur for himself, and ate it there.

A stiffish wind was blowing by the time he returned; the day began to cloud over. Peregrines love to play in the air in a wind; they love to show their mastery of it. The tiercel came back high, stooped near the lookout, and began a series of maneuvers that were breath-taking. At great speed he saw-toothed along the escarpment, rolled over and over, darted and flung himself about on the wind as a leaf is flung, and mounted straight up like a rocket leaving the earth to hang motionless for a second or two and plunge down again.

It is beautiful to see a living creature, mysteriously compounded of nerves and brain and tissue and pulsing blood, that is the master of the element in which it moves; beautiful to see the lightning swift co-ordination, the apparent wild reckless abandon that is not abandon but perfect control, and think of the spirit that moves it. In the peregrine it is a spirit of ice and fire, steely hard and burning, free in the high air; a wanderer, fearless and marvelously equipped to play with storms and great winds and do the killing that is its function and by which it lives. There is no streak of cruel feline playfulness in it; it kills quickly and surely, to satisfy its hunger.

The tiercel dropped to his stone, relaxed his feathers and settled them with a shake, and composed himself. He didn't sit still very long, however. Perhaps he knew, somewhere within him, that time was pressing upon them, that summer was coming in its brightness and would soon be over. He couldn't be passive, as the falcon was; there was an urgency upon him. It was an urgency that extended all around him, from the birds continually arriving from the south and establishing their territories and the lemmings running through their tunnels in the moss to the caribou in the Thelon Game Sanctuary several hundred miles to the west. The caribou had left the timber to the south where they had wintered and started across the soggy tundra on their long journey to their far northern calving grounds. Their calving had to be finished before snow came again, and although many of the bucks had dropped their many-tined, tall antlers, the does still had theirs.

The tiercel had to take the initiative; it was part of the pattern of his life. He wailed at the falcon and flew down to the old nesting site and wailed more, trying to entice her down. He soon left it and flew to another ledge, and another, to show her the wide choice of nesting places, scratching about on them and wailing at her as persuasively as he was able, but she wouldn't come.

It was several days before she began to show much interest in the ledges, although the tiercel spent more and more time on them, calling, between his hunting flights. Occasionally he would fly up near her, calling softly, and go back to them again. He took to standing on the front of one of them instead of on his stone, wailing once in a while, and sometimes she would answer him.

Presently, however, some of his excitement was communicated to her; her own rhythm was quickening. The spring sun's content of ultraviolet light, increasing as the northern pole of the earth swung more toward the sun, was strengthening the sway of its ancient magic upon her.

At first it had been only strong enough to cause the restlessness that started her north; but as she came up the coast, along the edge of the sea and across the flatlands and the great river estuaries, the coastal mountains and the plains to the south of Hudson Bay, the glandular change that it brought gave increasing purpose to her migration. She began to search for a tiercel, and when she saw the one on the Inlet came down to him. She had accepted him and his territory, his particular section of the precipitous and rocky section of cliffs along the Inlet. She had gone through the early stages of the courtship passively, his display flights and calling and moving about on the ledges; he had been ahead of her, but now she was catching up to him.

For the first time her interest in the ledges was aroused to the point where she jumped off the Inukok and flew down to join the tiercel. The pair of them moved about all over them, wailing and creaking like rusty hinges; they were like people arguing over an apartment or a house. The tiercel began to scratch about; the falcon flew to another ledge and soon the tiercel joined her and the argument started up again. Then the falcon left the ledge and flew back to the Inukok.

An observer would have thought that she had lost interest in house hunting, but she had not. Her return to the stone after looking at the ledges was as much a part of the pattern as the tiercel's flights before her were. It was a signal, an agreement; for after scratching about a bit more the tiercel flew up to the Inukok and they mated there, with low, soft, chuckling sounds that were never used at any other time. All the sounds they usually made when they were together (for at times other than the breeding season they were mostly silent birds) were rather harsh and certainly unmusical, but these were not.

They mated again in the early afternoon and would continue to do so daily until there was an egg or two on the chosen ledge. The tiercel soon began to lose his interest in nesting sites, spending more time in the air away from his stone; the falcon began investigating them in earnest. She was all over the cliffs on both sides of the Inlet, walking around on them, pushing herself into crevices and crawling into unlikely spots; on each ledge that she landed upon she would scratch about, puff herself up and lie down as though brooding, and twist and turn to get the feel of it. A sort of secretiveness took hold of her; a good deal of her activity went on while the tiercel was away, and she was very quiet with it. She moved from one place to another like a shadow, creeping from rock to rock when she was able; one would have thought that she was surrounded with enemies.

The ledge that she finally selected was two thirds of the way up the cliff, ten feet long and four feet wide, thrusting out from the cliff face into the air over the Inlet; it ran back from the face like a shallow cave dark and shadowed at the back, made darker by the heavy black filigree of a patch of lichen, *Parmelia sorediata,* on the rear wall. Being on the point of a curve it gave a view both ways; nothing could approach in either direction without being seen.

Having found a place to suit her she went busily to work on it, scratching out the frost-broken rock fragments until she had a smooth hollow that fitted her body and was an inch or two inches deep, and presently the first creamy egg, washed lightly with salmon pink and finely dotted with rich brown, was laid in it. Every other day another was laid, until there were four. For the first two weeks the tiercel did little of the brooding; the falcon sat closely on the eggs, only flying out to catch the food that the tiercel dropped to her from high in the air.

As the time drew out, however, the falcon relinquished her eggs to the tiercel more. She was too active a bird to bear almost complete inactivity for so long; even the old falconers knew that the long wings stiffened a little without exercise. She wanted to move about again, to feel once more the fierce joy of pursuit, and so in the middle of the morning and late in the afternoon she would sally out and the tiercel would cover the eggs.

Above the ledge, on the wide sweep of the Barrens, the snow disappeared and the land began to turn faintly green; the Arctic willow unrolled its fat pale green leaves and the silvery pussies shone on the low branches. Mountain mustard and cinquefoil and woolly lousewort and all the berries that snuggle down into the moss pushed up their buds toward the sun. There were innumerable secret nests around the innumerable ponds, and the air was filled with the voices of the nesters: northern phalarope and golden plover, whose cries seem so desolate and so lonely, oldsquaw ducks, white whistling swan with their loud, high-pitched, cooing *woo-ho! woo-ho!* the rolling trumpet call of red-capped sandhill cranes, and the cock ptarmigan's crow. Arctic terns flew about and piratical long-tailed jaegers robbed them; rough-legged hawks beat slowly back and forth above the ridges. Mosquitoes hatched from eggs deposited the autumn before in hollows where the melt water of spring would cover them arose in unbelievable clouds to search for blood. The silent land was not silent now, and the iron loneliness of winter was gone.

ARCTIC SUMMER

ON THE thirty-fourth day the first young hawk sawed its way through the shell with a patch of abrasive material on the forepart of its beak, called an egg-tooth, and emerged into the world. The egg-tooth had served its purpose and would soon disappear; the hawk, a small bit of protoplasm covered with wet down, was too weak to do anything but push feebly farther under its mother's warm feathers, and rest. Its eyes were not yet open and its neck would hardly hold up its heavy head.

Presently the falcon arose, looked closely at the new nestling, picked up the pieces of broken shell and dropped them over the lip of the ledge, and returned to settle herself carefully over it. The stir of life under her feathers gave an added alertness to her dark eyes; the somnolent time of brooding was nearly over. Later she heard the faint sounds above her as one of the big, pale Arctic wolves, working his way along the top of the escarpment, caught her scent and paused for a moment and went on.

Within the hour the tiercel returned from his wanderings; it was his hour for brooding, and he landed on the ledge. The day had been turning windy and overcast and cold, and the falcon made no move to get up and fly out. She was not going to leave the nestling. They clucked and talked to one another, creaking like rusty hinges, and presently the tiercel, knowing now that he was to do the hunting, dropped away from the ledge and flew off.

The other eggs hatched in their time and the nestlings in their fluffy white down grew stronger and their eyes opened; they sat on their bottoms, resting on their legs with their little bluish feet stuck out in front of them and looked brightly about. The falcon had started to hunt again, and until the young grew stronger and got on their feet they were fed with great care; when a bird was brought in by either of the parents they would tear it up and let the nestlings pick small pieces from the sides of their beaks.

The nestlings grew rapidly, and were soon scrambling about. At first they stayed at the rear of the ledge, but as they grew more adventurous they moved out and had many narrow escapes from falling into the Inlet far below. They found their voices and the ledge, which had been comparatively quiet when they were so small, became a noisy place. When either of the parents flew in with a bird, giving the food call, they would all start screaming and scrambling over one another to get to it first. As they grew and their new feathers began to push through the down their feeding times became ever more noisy and riotous. They were always famished; the single goal of their lives was to snatch the next morsel that appeared, make off into a corner with it, get it under them and gulp it down before someone else got it; there were loud and desperate battles all over the ledge. The two old birds sometimes took to not landing on the ledge at all. The spirit of playfulness which peregrines have, suppressed in the pair for so long by their concentration upon mating and nesting, was beginning to emerge again. With a bird in their talons they would glide, calling, back and forth a few feet from the ledge's lip teasing the young ones, which would all dance about screaming with frustration and almost falling off the edge with eagerness; and finally they would fly closer, roll to one side, cast their prey on the ledge as they passed and let the battle go on without them.

Two of the young birds were tiercels and smaller than their sisters, but they were livelier; they were up and down the ledge twice as often but usually toward the back. They were much alike in all they did, but the two young falcons were dissimilar. The lighter colored of the two was very active and frequently ran about with the tiercels; she developed a sort of playfulness early and would often strike out at small stones on the ledge or take up a picked bone in her beak, toss it to one side or the other and follow it to pick it up again. The other, except at feeding time, was rather quiet and, in comparison with the other three, almost morose. She liked to sit hunched near the lip of the ledge and look up and down the Inlet, and would do it for long periods. Her withdrawal from the activity of the ledge seemed somehow to have an air of melancholy about it, and there may have been some somber prescience within her that urged her to see as much of her world as she could before she left it; for she was marked for death.

She was sitting there one day when a large female snowy owl, wandering about because she was unmated and so without a territory, happened to be flying a line that crossed the Inlet immediately above the ledge. The owl was hungry; the young falcon moved a little just as she cleared the escarpment and her cold yellow eyes caught the movement. The hair-trigger response that all hunting birds must have checked her forward movement on the instant; she twisted in the air, the five foot wings closed, and she slid across the ledge like a ghost and picked up the young falcon. All eight of the needle-sharp black talons were driven into the falcon by the owl's terrible grip; one of them penetrated all the way through her heart and she died at once.

The old falcon, returning just below the escarpment down the Inlet with a ptarmigan in her foot, saw the owl as it cleared the rocks above the ledge. Even before it had seized the fledgling she had dropped the ptarmigan and put on her best speed. Her long wings sang upon the air; she drew in on the pale, gliding owl like a slaty Nemesis. She rose a little as she neared it and then angled down to gain even more speed, dropping the hind talon of her foot, which caught the owl at the base of its skull as she went over it. Her speed and the power of her blow were so great that the owl's skull was split. It rolled over and fell into the Inlet below, leaving a few white feathers to float slowly down through the air.

Only then did the falcon cry her rage and triumph; her *kak! kak! kak! kak!* echoed around the gorge. She turned upward in the air momentarily and then dropped to the ledge. The whole thing had happened so quickly that the young birds, startled by the owl's swoop, were still in their posture of defense with their backs against the rear wall. Their heads were low and their eyes were menacing; their feathers were standing out to make them look larger, and they were ready to throw themselves onto their backs and present their talons to an attacker. They looked slightly ridiculous, half-grown and patched with white down, scattered and growing dark feathers still down-tipped with little points of white, but their spirit wasn't ridiculous; it had been their first brush with trouble, and they were prepared to give a good account of themselves.

They were reassured by her return; they relaxed their feathers, and forgetting their recent narrow escape ran screaming toward her for food. She clucked to them, surveyed the ledge, looked up and down the Inlet, and took to the air. As she rose above the escarpment she remembered the ptarmigan she had dropped, and went down to look for it.

The young hawks feathered out and began to exercise their wings, for the quills of their wing and tail feathers hardened as a buck's antlers harden beneath the velvet and become ready for use; they stood on the ledge and flapped their wings up and down. They were becoming impatient with being bound to the earth, and soon would be ready for the air.

The short, bright Arctic summer burgeoned around them: mountain mustard with its spidery white petals, yellow buttercups, woolly lousewort red-pink with its fluffy white balls that are called Arctic cotton, starred the pale green or lilac of the caribou moss which was deep and resilient under foot. Arctic bell heather flowered in the damp hollows and under muddy banks; cloudberry, crowberry and cranberry swelled toward ripening the fruits which were larger than the tiny bushes that bore them, Vaccinium covering the hillsides nourished in profusion the blueberries which when ripened would glow with the lovely bloom of purple grapes, and Polytrichum thrust up in delicate crimson. On the glacial gray rocks and in their crevices the lichens, working patiently with rain and frost to change the hard granite to dust, flamed with silver and orange, purple and gold, lilac, pale olive, ghostly white and scarlet, making thin soil for the mosses that followed them and glowed with color like Oriental rugs. Almost all of these things were very low-growing and small, but in a land called barren they made a miniature garden whose colors and extent and complexity would be incredible to an eye accustomed to the tall and riotous greenery of the south.

The cheek pockets of the lemmings and ground squirrels bulged with seeds for their storehouses, and the little creatures themselves fell prey to the foxes and weasels, snowy owls and rough-legged hawks. The caribou, drifting back from their calving grounds, followed by white wolves and occasionally encountering a wolverine, moved constantly against the wind in an endeavor to escape the warble flies that whined around them. On the tundra a number of the smaller ponds had dried up but the larger ones still reflected the blue of the sky and the flicker of a multitude of wings; the voices of plover and cranes, swans and ducks and lesser Canada geese, buntings and longspurs accompanied the snowy owls' ventriloquial hollow booming and the goblin hilarity of the loons.

THE WIDE SKY

A SUBTLE CHANGE began in the rhythm of the northern world as bright summer moved toward its end; berries ripened and grasses dropped their seeds on the wind and began to turn golden brown. The endless day was endless no longer; it darkened at midnight, and every day brought a little more of the night. Some of the smaller birds were already on the wing and moving about, and even among the nest-bound a stirring of restlessness awoke and ran along the nerves. It was not an urgency yet but was building toward urgency, as though they had an intimation not yet strong or complete that the sun and its warmth and light was leaving them and they would presently have to follow it toward the south. The Arctic char, those cousins to the brook trout, moved up the streams into still lakes where they would spawn and spend the winter; the males were brilliant with red bellies and orange spots on their sides.

The young hawks were ready to fly now; their long primaries and flight and tail feathers were hard-summed and stiff and their juvenile plumage was complete. They didn't look like their parents and wouldn't until their first molt was over in a year or so. Their backs, wings, and tails were dark brown instead of slaty; instead of gray striped horizontally with black the tiercels' breasts were pale cinnamon barred vertically with brown. The young falcon, which we shall call Varda now because we shall follow her, was a lighter bird; she was the golden one. The brown on her accentuated her brilliance; she had almost a golden gleam in the sun. Her moustache mark stood out strongly, and even on the crown of her head the tiny golden feathers were scattered through the dark and showed an intricate and beautiful pattern like the finest Damascene work. The skin on all their legs and feet, their ceres, and around their eyes was pale cerulean; good feeding and sunshine would turn it butter-yellow in time.

Beside her darker brothers the falcon, Varda, stood out because of her color and her size; she was also the most independent of the three. Her personality had been formed sooner and was more complete; she began to long for the air before they did. Exercising her wing muscles, she was rising a foot or two above the floor of the ledge before they thought of getting their feet off the rock, and it wasn't going to be necessary for the old birds to entice her into the air. The moment she felt ready for it, when her desire grew sufficient to overcome the nestling's instinctive fear of empty space, she walked to the ledge's lip and launched herself. Neither of the old birds was about; she didn't need them.

She dipped a little, and wobbled in the air. All the nestling's terror of falling washed over her. The water in the Inlet ran glittering below, moving and insubstantial, not like the steady rock. She had a moment of fear, the foundations of the world had gone from under her; and then her instinctive reaction, the nerves' ancient ancestral memories of flight, took over and steadied her. Her tail spread to give her buoyancy, her wings moved, and as she gained forward speed her balance returned and she swiftly gained more control of herself in the new element.

The cliffs opposite the ledge, the eyrie, were rushing toward her and she wasn't prepared to land on them. She banked away, clumsily, and swung a wide and rather uncertain half circle which brought her back to the eyrie side. The turn had slowed her, but as she was learning the intricate mechanics of flight very quickly she managed to land in good order on a lower rock jutting from the cliff face. Once on the rock she was proud of herself; she moved about excitedly, bowing and clucking in self-congratulation. The tiercels, who had been watching with great interest, yelled at her from above and the old falcon, coming in with a bird in her foot, added her voice to the chorus as she landed on the ledge. Varda talked back to them, her excitement rising as the realization of the delights of being no longer ledge-bound strengthened within her. She picked out another rock and flew to it, and then another. As her confidence increased and her instinct helped her, as she learned quickly to cope with the breeze and the shifting air currents and to manage herself, she made longer flights, turned and climbed and took increasing joy in the air and its freedom.

Late in the afternoon she landed on the ledge, to be welcomed again by the tiercels and their father. She was tired and hungry, but there was a new look about her and a new bearing. Her rightful world lay now just beyond the ledge's lip and she was what the falconers, who through the centuries have built up a vocabulary for their sport, call a *passager*, because she was on the wing and soon to make the passage of her first migration.

Now that one of their young was on the wing the old birds (called *haggards* by falconers, from the Hebrew word "hagar," meaning *wild*) began maneuvering to get the other two into the air. As though by agreement they stopped bringing food to the ledge. They came in off the Barrens with prey, giving the feeding call and flying back and forth almost within reach, but not landing; then they would fly across the Inlet and perch on a rock in plain view. The tiercels screamed and danced about; they ran to the edge, opened their wings, almost launched themselves and then hurriedly scrambled back. The next day one of them became so recklessly impatient that he tumbled off the ledge and had to fly. He made it to the other side and was fed, but it was two more days before the other trusted himself to the air.

Now they were all launched and in a few days seemed to fly as well as their parents, and a happy time began for them. They were still a family, they all went back to the ledge or near it to roost at night, and their parents fed them by dropping dead birds that they caught in the air or flew past them with prey that the young, rolling sideways, snatched from their talons. They began to hunt for themselves, at first not very successfully, and to play.

One of them, high in the blue, would fold his wings and stoop at another; the other would shift with wild wails, they would seem to merge for an instant, separate, and plunge downward together ripping the air, race to climb one above another and go through their mock battle again. The third would join them and they would fling themselves about, roll and plunge like meteors and bound upward, soar for a while and then engage once more. Sometimes they would fly slowly and directly at one another with shallow wingbeats, meet screaming and clasp talons, roll about and break away again. Frequently one or both of the haggards, with the finish and superior style of long experience, would join the play and show them that they weren't finished flyers yet.

Varda had this experience. She was very high; she had found a good updraft and been carried up on it, soaring, until she was invisible from the earth. It seemed that she was far above them all, alone in the silence of the sky, until her retina caught a stir of movement and she cocked her head and found the old tiercel her father high above her. He was circling lazily, but from his lofty pitch he controlled her; he could stoop on her when he liked. She drifted away, from under him, and he swung with her; she drifted more and he swung ahead of her and brought her back. She started to climb to cut his advantage and he climbed above her faster.

As this game went on excitement built in her; she would elude him yet. She started to descend a little to put more space between them, and he flashed over and gave several swift wingbeats as though to stoop. She was caught by this maneuver, forgetting that she could shift and dodge much better in level flight; she rolled over at once, gave six swift wingbeats, folded her wings and plunged straight toward the earth.

The tiercel rolled again and came after her, but his wings didn't stop beating. They increased their rhythm, slashing at the air. He was flying vertically downward as hard as he was able, picking up a speed that was already well over two hundred miles an hour, and he rapidly overhauled her, while the wind of their reckless and beautiful plunge roared past. The tiercel drew inexorably in, swept across her back, tapped her lightly with one closed fist and turned upward, crying his triumph. With half-opened wings he scudded vertically toward heaven, and took his station again.

*

Beneath the Olympian play of the hawks the Vaccinium was turning to crimson and the grasses to somber gold; the lemmings were carrying more bedding into their burrows against the coming cold and the ptarmigan showed a scattering of new white feathers. The boggy places where the mosses grew and thrust up their glowing colors were being leached of color, and the long, downlike hills were often dark with shadows, for clouds and overcast were more frequent now. A foreboding chill came into the air, and soon there was in some places a light dusting of snow which the waning and infrequent sun took away by noon. The birds were beginning to leave, some to go no farther south than the timber at the edge of the Barrens and some to fly thousands of miles to the Chesapeake, the southern Atlantic beaches, the shores of the Gulf of Mexico, South America, or the Antarctic. Geese and swans and ducks traded restlessly about, gabbling together and slowly moving south, reluctant to leave the familiar grounds of summer but impelled to go.

One of the young tiercels still followed his mother and begged to be fed, wailing at her; he was the lazy one. The other ranged more widely and was killing small birds for himself; Varda ranged more widely still. The family tie that had held them all together, and given them such excellent training and flying proficiency by their play, was almost gone in her now. She had always been the least dependent of them, the first to try a new thing, and the urge to be away, to take up her solitary course, increased every day. The peregrine is by nature a wanderer, and although it has a pattern of migration it does not always keep rigidly to it; it is such a swift flyer that time and distance impose less necessity upon it than does the necessity of finding prey, and Varda felt no great urge for the south yet. Her breast was round as an apple with good feeding; the bloom of health was on her feathers, and her abounding energy was no longer satisfied with flights centered around the ledge and the country she knew so well.

The first light snow to fall in the vicinity of the eyrie sifted softly down onto the ledge before sunrise, and Varda felt it on her feathers; she woke to wonder at it, for it was different from rain. It blew around her feet a little in the first wan daylight, pale, almost as fluid as water, and she looked at it carefully and walked about in it; she pecked at it, and it turned to water in her mouth. She shook her head, looked up and down the shadowy Inlet, and dropped off the edge. This was the day she was to go; she rose on the wind above the ledge and the escarpment, circled, wailed at the others and straightened to the east.

Several miles down the Inlet she came out of a drift of low cloud and saw a late phalarope, which had been delayed by a wing injury, beneath her and stooped at it. The bird dropped for the gorge but she slid beneath it, rolled over onto her back and caught it with one extended foot as she passed under it. She took it to the escarpment, landed upon another Inukok there, and plucked and ate it. She cleaned her beak on the stone and took off again. The sun was up by now, red in the east and coloring the broken clouds, and she flew on toward it.

She mounted higher and the country opened out beneath her and far to the sides; the gorge dropped behind her and the Inlet widened out and the Quoich River opened into it. All around like an immense bowl the sweep of bare rolling hills, the rocky distant escarpments and the lakes moved out to the horizon, dun and old gold and lovely varied crimson where the great areas of Vaccinium made their final stand against the frost. From her height she could see six local snowstorms widely scattered around the land and great areas of thin sunshine; and then she saw the ship.

It was the Hudson's Bay Company supply ship steaming up the Inlet to the Company post at Baker Lake, on its annual trip of collection and supply, and she had never seen anything like it before. It moved in the water, and a thin wisp of smoke came from the stack; with its masts and rigging and deckhouses and black and white paint it was alien and strange, and she dropped down and circled it several times at masthead height to look at it. Several men were moving about on deck and there were two more sitting on the wheelhouse roof; one of them raised his binoculars at once to look at her. If Varda had been a haggard, an older and more experienced and suspicious bird, she would have gone off at once; indeed, it is doubtful that she would have approached the ship at all. She could not have known that the man with binoculars was a falconer, devotee of an archaic sport once followed by nobility and commoner alike before the introduction of gunpowder and the shotgun. There are not many falconers now because hawks are so difficult to trap and train and maintain in proper hunting condition; but a few people like hawks so well and derive so much satisfaction from watching them fly that they accept the challenge. Perhaps most of them are rebels or romantics, who like to ally themselves with the more colorful days of the Middle Ages, when falconry was at its height: the pageantry and the costumes, the setting forth on horseback with dogs and servants to roam over country uncluttered by the works of man, the sport and the return to the manor house.

The falconer didn't consciously think of this while he had Varda in the binoculars; he longed for her. Her golden color was a delight, and although he had seen a number of peregrines as they came up the Inlet none of them had flown in and circled the ship to look at it. They had perched immobile on rocks on the skyline or flown off at the ship's approach, and Varda's curiosity as well as her striking color set her apart. He watched her as she swung off to the east again, and put the binoculars down on the wheelhouse roof. "Ah, she was handsome," he said to himself. "She was wonderful. I wish I had her."

VARDA SETS OUT

PRESENTLY Varda flew into the edge of a snowstorm, and not liking it turned northward into clear air; half an hour later she encountered another, and dropped down to perch on a high rock on a hilltop which the storm had just passed. Farther to the north, small in the distance, she could see a herd of caribou. They were moving westward to pass

to the north of Baker Lake and drop down toward the Thelon River and the treeline where they would winter. They were led by an old buck whose antlers were grown and hardened now; he would trot ahead, pause to feed a little, and start out again when the rest of the herd caught up with him. When they were all bunched their tall, many-branched antlers made them look like a thicket on the march. The mosquitoes that had kept them trotting into the wind all summer were gone now, they were all more or less footsore from their long journey out of the north, and were not hurrying much. Four big Arctic wolves were following them, lazily and at a distance, and would make a kill toward evening. The wolves lived mainly on caribou, and not having speed enough to catch them in a straight-away chase usually arranged a sort of surround. Three of them would hide at different strategic points and the remaining one would drive a caribou toward them. This did not always work, but it worked often enough to keep the wolves in good condition.

In the middle of the afternoon Varda took to the air again; the wind was behind her, and she paralleled the course that the caribou had taken. She passed high over several long vees of Canada geese which cocked their heads and talked together as she went over them. They would spend a few days at Baker Lake and then work their way down to James Bay, across to the St. Lawrence, and south to the Atlantic coast. They would spend the winter at Currituck, what was left of them, after they ran the long gantlet of goose pits already being prepared for the hunters who would wait for them.

Late in the afternoon Varda reached Baker Lake and flew along the north shore until she could see the Hudson's Bay Company post and the radiosonde mast near the end of the Lake. There were many sled dogs tied up but rather few people about, and most of the latter were Eskimo women and children; practically all of the men had gone north, inland, to shoot caribou on the migration. Many of the hides taken would go on the ship to Lake Harbour and Frobisher Bay and Cape Dorset, for they made the warmest winter parkas — double, with one skin facing in and the other out — and caribou were very scarce on Baffin Island.

The falcon circled high above the little settlement, so small and lonely between the vast sweep of rolling tundra and the Lake; the store and the manager's house with the walk between them bordered by white painted stones, the chapel and the Royal Canadian Mounted Police building, the weather station with its radio mast and the Eskimo tents which would soon be struck as their owners left for their winter trapping grounds. It was as new and strange to her as the ship had been, and now that she had seen it her instinct to beware of unknown things warned her away from it, although she wanted to land now. She swung away from it and looked for a high stone because there were no cliffs within her view; at some distance down the Lake she finally found an Eskimo grave, built above ground with flat stones because of the iron-hard permafrost, and landed on its lichened top.

Presently a flock of golden plover, flying low and together and following the contour of the ground, came down the Lake shore. Varda was off the grave in a flash, and flying fast and low behind a rise appeared among them and had one almost before they knew she was there. The flock, crying their fear, scattered and rose; Varda returned to the grave with her prey and plucked and ate it.

The sun went down and the sky above the western hills turned pale, pellucid green. An Arctic weasel, attracted by the scent of plover's blood, bounded across the reindeer moss and paused with one foot upheld; its mad eyes burned as it looked at the falcon. Varda puffed out her feathers and hissed at it, and it bounded off. Varda shook herself and settled down for the night; her first day away from the eyrie was over.

She was one of many species of birds on the Lake and around it, stopping in for a few days to feed and rest before taking up their long journey to the south. Some of them had already flown far, from the Arctic coast and the shores of the Beaufort Sea and the bleak islands above it, from McClintock Channel and Barrow Strait. They were a small segment of the millions that were funneling down from the top of the continent, from sea to sea, on the vast and mysterious march that has puzzled and fascinated man for nearly three thousand years, some to move across the Canadian prairies and the Great Lakes to Chesapeake Bay, others to take the path of the Mississippi to the Gulf or farther south. These were the great eastern flyways, the paths of most of them, but the Arctic terns of the eastern Arctic took their own pathway down Hudson Strait and the north and south Atlantic, sometimes by way of Africa, to the Antarctic. Some traveled at night, in the darkness without landmarks, or over the trackless ocean. No man knew for a surety what guided them, any more than he knew why the golden plover from Alaska flew nonstop over the Pacific to Hawaii while those from the eastern Arctic traveled from Nova Scotia down the lonely Atlantic to Brazil.

For a few days Varda was content to stay in the vicinity of Baker Lake, with the short Indian summer. Her urge to get away, to wander about over the land, was quieted for the moment, and the large area of water, its small waves sparkling in the sun in a running and intricate pattern when the wind stirred them, satisfied something within her after the dark, narrow gorge of the Inlet. Like all of her race she was happiest when there was broad water within her view, and not only because most of the birds on which she lived frequented it. All that the place needed was a great precipitous cliff or a tall mountaintop stone; peregrines love the highest spot they can find, where the sweep of the world is beneath them.

She spent much time soaring, when there was enough sunshine to warm the earth and bring rising currents of air off it; only glider pilots among men could share with her the joy of that silent, effortless roaming, borne up by the power that comes from the sun, high above the loons and the geese, the ducks and pale gulls and somber ravens going about their concerns and the roughlegs patrolling the tundra. Once a merlin, that lively miniature falcon, pursued a bird into her realm, checked off it and cried at her and she stooped at it in play. They maneuvered in the high air with breath-taking shifts and plunges until they tired of their sport and the merlin went off again, twisting and crying his pleasure at her.

Once, moving for a way up the Thelon River, she saw a gathering of herring gulls on the bank and lowered her pitch and circled them. There was a dead caribou at the edge of the water; it had drowned in a stretch of rapids as it was crossing the River and washed down, and the gulls had gathered to feast upon it. Ordinarily they were quarrelsome birds, fighting one another viciously for the fish that they caught, but here they were as orderly and circumspect as a gathering of deacons. They ringed the caribou and each gull stepped forth in his turn and filled his crop with meat while the others waited.

Weather turned gray at the Lake; a thick overcast moved across the sky and threatened to remain, and Varda grew restless again. She moved northwest, flying low, and then west. Two days later she was in the Thelon Sanctuary where she saw the first scattering of spruces and her first musk ox along the River. There were twelve in the herd, which was moving in a leisurely fashion toward higher ground for the winter. The big beasts, weighing as much as eight hundred pounds, which seemed to like bleak country as well as the snow buntings liked it, whose long, thick fur kept them warm in any weather, had been nearly exterminated by Indians, Eskimos and trappers before the Sanctuary had been set aside for them. Once they had been able to protect themselves well from wolves and Barren Grounds grizzlies by forming a line or circle of horns from which the bulls sallied out against attackers. Their ancient defense had finally betrayed them; for when men came with their dogs the musk ox had stood lined up against them and repeating rifles found them easy targets. Slow breeders, they were much reduced in numbers; they were safe only in the Sanctuary now and seemed to know it.

The weather stayed sunless and chill, with gray days and fiery broken sunsets, and the land turned its face toward winter. The Barrens, which had been so filled with life, so bright with low-growing flowers and song and the flicker of wings, retreated toward dun-colored silence and snow, a stillness broken only by the disembodied march of the northern lights across the sky and the long howls of the wolves.

The Arctic foxes stored a portion of their catches against the harder times to come, and the last birds were leaving. Varda turned toward the southeast. Almost at once a storm overtook her. She had experienced a number of storms in her short life, riding and tumbling about on them with a wild joy, but none had been like this one. The somber day turned nearly as black as night, the wind's wail deepened to a roar, and the sleet that came with it was driven nearly horizontally, hissing like bullets. Every living thing got out of its way and found a sheltered cranny to crouch in, and Varda was forced to join them; she could do nothing against the ferocity of the elements. She found a small, cavelike hollow between two great glacial rocks and was fairly blown into it, out of the blinding sleet. She didn't like the enclosing walls of the place, which met several feet over her head and cut off any view or avenue of retreat to her rear; it was against all her instincts to be confined; but she had no choice and was at least sheltered for the moment.

The storm continued for the rest of the day and through the night and most of the next day. Varda sat through it, dozing fitfully, with feathers puffed out. It was nearly dark when it was over, and the wind was still strong. The world was covered with ice that glittered coldly in the failing spears of light that filtered through the cloud wrack when Varda was driven from her shelter by hunger and dislike of her situation. Nothing was moving within her view except a weasel, which had caught her scent and was bounding toward her. He was hungry enough to attack her and intended to do it, for these mad little creatures have no inhibiting sense of fear when they are hungry and a disparity in size means nothing to them; they have been known to attack moose. Varda, on her part, was hungry enough to attack him, but she didn't do it directly. She jumped into the air and flew over him, gaining height. He leaped up at her, fell far short, and turned away; she swung off and into the wind, turned, and with it behind her swept after him. He had already forgotten her, having missed her, and was bounding away. She reached him; her feet came out with lightning quickness; four talons closed on his head and four sank into the middle of his back, and she had him stretched and powerless. She landed, and as he writhed and screamed with rage and pain she broke his neck, and ate him.

Now that the battering sleet was over and she had fed she wanted to get away from the place that had confined her; an aversion to it ran along her nerves; and although darkness was falling she jumped into the air to find a better perching place. Peregrines see fairly well in dim light, unlike a number of hawks, and within half an hour she found a high stone with a shoulder to keep off most of the wind and landed on it.

The morning dawned clear, with gauzy veils of mist near the ground, and Varda was in the air with the first light. The urge to move south, which had been quickening in her before the storm, was strong now. It was like the pull of the north on the compass needle, and drew her toward the lands of the sun. She was hungry, but didn't turn aside to hunt; she would hunt as the opportunity presented itself on her course. She flew just high enough to clear the mist, at the swift and purposeful pace of a peregrine on migration; her course took her a little north of the treeline that angled roughly from Churchill to the north of Great Bear Lake.

This was mostly muskeg country, studded with lakes and with a few islands of spruce that had managed to maintain themselves in it, crossed by streams and rather devoid of prey because most of the migrant birds had already passed through it. Her wanderings about the Sanctuary had made her a little late and her appetite was sharp set before she came upon three scaup which rose through the ground mist lying over the river in front of her. Ducks look large to young peregrines and they do not usually begin to prey upon them until later in the fall when they have gained more confidence in themselves, but Varda didn't hesitate. She picked out the drake as the three scattered, quacking their alarm, and caught him as he dove down toward the mist again.

Well fed, she bathed in a little backwater at the edge of the river from which the ducks had arisen. There was a skim of ice around the edges of it. She spent an hour on the shore with her wings extended in the intermittent sunlight to dry herself, and took up her way again.

Late the next afternoon she came off the Barrens near the mouth of the Caribou River, and the wide sweep of Hudson Bay opened before her. She found an open stretch of beach where she could see all around her, and came down for the night. She was at the edge of civilization; Churchill was not far away. In the morning she would see it; and although it was a remote and lonely outpost, five hundred miles at the end of the railroad line from the nearest city to the south, it was the beginning of man's dominion. From now on, unless her fate returned her to the Barrens again, she would never be free of his shadow or his power.

LAND OF SHADOWS

A SCHOOL of white whales, pale arrows flying beneath the rippled surface of the blue water, were moving south off-shore as Varda flew from the beach. She circled to look down at them, and went on. They would lose part of their number to Eskimo hunters near the mouth of the Churchill River; rifles and harpoons would take toll of them for winter dog food, for the whale processing plant in the town was closed now.

She crossed Churchill at about five hundred feet, having found a little wind at that altitude which favored her. It was the first town she had ever seen, and it was a small one, its low houses scattered about on the muddy streets and its

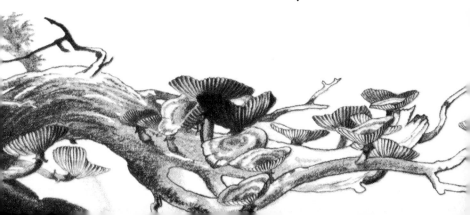

grain elevator standing like a great rectangular white rock above them. It had been settled in the seventeenth century as the trading and supply center of the northeastern fur trade, which had been a rich one; the French and English had fought over it, and then its importance had declined. It was now mostly a shipping center for wheat from the prairie provinces, but the harbor was used only in the two summer months between freeze-up and break-up of the ice, and the last grain ship had loaded and gone. The elevator would soon close down for the winter and the people who operated it would move south until the ice went out again. The Hudson's Bay Company supply ship from which the falconer and his companion had seen Varda had left from here to supply the northern posts; she would not return to Churchill but to Montreal. The Chipewyan Indians who lived in town in summer were preparing to move out to their winter trapping territories, and the people who would stay were preparing for temperatures down to fifty-five degrees below zero and the bitter winter winds from the Barrens.

The lonely little town fell behind the falcon; she flew on overland until she crossed the Bay at the foot of which Port Nelson and the old York Factory fur post were located and came out over the Hudson Bay shoreline again. The weather, which had been cloudy and gray when she started, grew brighter. East of Churchill she had come to the tree-line; the massed spires of the spruces were below her now, their somber darkness relieved by small patches of crimson and gold which glowed when the strengthening sunshine found them and made the world less desolate. The increasing brightness of the day lifted Varda's spirits and eased in her the feeling for the necessity of haste. Also, the forest interested her. She had never seen its like before; so much was hidden under it that in her birthplace had lain open to the sky. While she didn't know that different creatures — mink and marten, fisher and beaver and lynx — lived in it, she was cautious; she didn't trust what she couldn't see; and presently, to rest and get a better look at it, she landed on one of the topmost branches of a tall, lightning-blasted spruce.

A few ducks were moving out on the Bay. She watched them with interest; hunger was coming upon her, but she wasn't ready to go after one of them yet. The sun felt pleasant; she dozed for a few minutes, and woke to see a tawny movement below her. It was a lynx, that long-legged cat with a stumpy tail and tufted ears. Like a shadow it moved on its big paws along the trunk of a down tree and surveyed the shoreline. It was a creature new to her, and looked as though it could be troublesome; it confirmed her suspicions of the concealing trees, and she croaked at it. The lynx looked up, somewhat shamefaced that it had been observed, curled its upper lip to show gleaming teeth, and slid out of sight as silently as it had come.

She shook herself and turned her attention to the Bay again. Presently, far out, she saw an osprey drop from the sky, hit the water with a splash, and beat into the air again with a fish in its talons. The spirit of play, which had been repressed by the cold and sleet and gray skies, by the urge to get away from them, awoke in her again. She dropped from the limb and flew toward the osprey, which soon saw her coming and began to ring up into the sky. She ascended faster; presently she was above it, and from her pitch swung lazily to and fro to shepherd it as the whim took her. The osprey, a much larger bird began to cry its protest, and tried to make for the shore. Varda let it go a little way, and stooped; the osprey rolled over on its back and thrust up one taloned foot, but it was not Varda's intention to close with it. She turned upward again three or four feet above the crying osprey, and stooped again as soon as it had righted itself. She continued this maneuver, greatly enjoying herself, and the osprey lost height at every encounter until she had it standing, frustrated and protesting loudly, on the beach; then she flew off.

She went on, to take a duck and feed on it, and roosted for the night in another dead spruce on the shore not many miles from the Severn post of the Hudson's Bay Company. To the south of her, scattered through the wooded country of rivers and lakes, there were many posts which had a long history in the fur trade: Big Beaver House, Lansdowne House, Windigo Lake, Ogoki, Nakina, Ghost River, Long Lac, and others — Indian, French, and English names, enduring evidence of the men who for several hundred years had lived in hardship and loneliness to follow their trap-lines in the cold and the snow, dying alone or often being

on the edge of death; the French and the half-breeds sing-
ing their songs in the wilderness, the silent Indians moving
on their webs through the snowy gloom of the spruces, and
the English, the traders, often living in some comfort and
state in their trading posts. There had often been debauches
and cruelty, thievery and violence and mean and greedy
conniving in the trade, but there had also been splendid
endurance and sacrifice and great feats almost beyond the
seeming strength of men; the stuff of legends had been in it.

Taking up her way again, Varda continued along the
shore and turned to follow the shoreline down into James
Bay. The impenetrable spruce forest still blanketed the
land and concealed all the life that moved about within it
but as she moved farther south, toward Moose Factory and
the foot of James Bay, the life upon the water greatly
increased. From Baffin Island, Foxe Basin, and the eastern
shore of Hudson Bay, from a thousand miles to the northward, the birds which had spent the summer and raised
their young were funneling down. There were ducks and
a multitude of smaller birds; Canada geese from the rivers
and lakes of Quebec's western shore and blue geese from
Foxe Basin. The main body of snow geese, which held
pretty well together, had gone on to the St. Lawrence to
stay there in their white companies for several months, but
there were a few late stragglers with the blues. They would
all leave presently for the coastal marshes of Louisiana,
going down the Mississippi Valley, but the Canadas would

turn east for the Atlantic or angle down across the mountains for Chesapeake Bay and Currituck.

There was no need for Varda to hurry for the moment; there was plenty for her to live upon, and once more she hesitated in her journey and wandered casually about a little while in a world that was new to her. She watched the play of life and pursued her prey and learned a little about men. One day, soaring high over a strangely motionless flock of geese on the water near shore, she watched another flock coming from the north swing under her, talking in chorus, and set their wings to join the motionless ones. When they were close the hunters stood up in their blind and their guns blasted like sharp thunder. Five geese folded in the air and dropped and then the men came out and picked them up. Death in this way was a strange and mysterious thing, but it was death; and the tall, erect creatures had had a part in it.

Varda couldn't know that they had brought the bison, the whooping crane and the Eskimo curlew to the edge of extinction and pushed the passenger pigeon and the heath hen beyond it, that these creatures which had once seemed inexhaustible in their millions were gone and that others would probably follow them before men desired them alive more than dead, but she swung away. The lesson would stay with her now; she was fortunate that she had become aware of man and his destructive capabilities at a distance, that what she had seen would now strengthen her inborn blind and instinctive distrust of him. Too many of her species would learn this lesson as a charge of shot broke them up and brought them out of the air simply because they were hawks, or a difficult target, or because the gunner justified himself by thinking that he was acting as a public benefactor. She would never consciously get close to him again, and barring the accident of surprise would be free of him so long as her life lasted; but his works went far beyond him, and against this she had no defense.

For the few days that the good weather held, Varda wandered around the southern shore of James Bay. There was more color in the country now as she got closer to the transition zone, more autumn gold to relieve the darkness of the spruces, and she encountered several other peregrines that had come down from the western shore of Baffin Island. The young ones like herself were curious and still felt the need of company occasionally, having such a short time ago left their families. When they saw her, or when she saw them, they would approach one another in the air, circle and talk a little before separating again. The older birds, the haggards, were used to solitude and preferred it; they had worked hard during the summer to raise young, and wanted to be free of them. They were not morose; few peregrines are; but they liked their privacy and were quite ready to enforce it, and after a single experience with one of them, when she tried to perch companionably in the same tree and was driven off, Varda let them alone.

She was not discomfited by this encounter; it was merely

a part of her education. She had learned that the haggards could still outfly and outmaneuver her, and she went on her way. Several days later, on a morning when a cold mist lay over the water, its top a little below her perch, she launched herself and circled up to a high pitch. The mist rolled beneath her, pale and restless, reflecting the clear sky above and shot with the colors of sunrise to the east, and presently a wind from the north came up. She began to soar on it, rising higher and higher, stretching the long axis of each ellipse toward the south, leaving the Bay behind her. In the high, cool silence and the sun the joy of soaring had an almost hypnotic effect upon her; the hours went by as she was buoyed up and carried on her way, seeing another occasional migrant far below, the lakes and the winding rivers, the woods concealing their secret and hidden lives.

In the afternoon a cloud bank with its threat of shifty turbulence brought her lower; she dropped to treetop height and began to fly, keeping a sharp watch as hunger overtook her. The sky cleared again as she traveled, but she stayed low. The openings in the trees became more frequent, with rocky outcrops, as the country began to roll a little; she flew over an ungainly moose browsing in one of them and as she came into another a grouse sunning itself on top of a pile of stones was so startled by her sudden appearance that it flushed and flew for the trees. She was going so fast that she overhauled it before it could reach them; she struck it a paralyzing blow with her closed foot, knocked it stunned to the ground, turned in the air and dropped on it before it could recover again. Although she didn't like the encircling trees, which closed her in, she plumed it and began to eat, raising her head frequently to look about. When she was partway through the grouse a flicker of wings at the edge of the clearing caught her eye. As she looked up a goshawk landed on the pile of stones where the grouse had been sunning itself.

Varda, although she had never seen a goshawk, recognized the gray bird at once as a deadly enemy; its orange-red eyes, so brilliant that the ancient Greeks called it "the starry-eyed one," burned upon Varda and her quarry. It would have attacked at once if Varda's size hadn't equaled its own. Although it was strong, swift and fearless, supremely maneuverable in the tangled brush of its domain, the goshawk had recognized Varda as a dangerous opponent and paused to consider. Varda, at a great disadvantage on the ground, stared back menacingly, ready at the goshawk's slightest movement to throw herself on her back and bring her talons into play.

For a long moment the two birds stared at one another in the silence while probable death for both of them stood in the balance, then the goshawk decided to avoid conflict. It screamed a rapid, harsh, threatening *cac! cac! cac!* and jumped from the stones, turned in its own length, and vanished into the spruces again. After a long period of watchfulness Varda finished the grouse and flew up into a dead tree to sleep for the night.

A new moon came up with the darkness and brought a

fox to investigate the carcass of the grouse; Varda could hear it crunching the bones that she had left. Toward midnight a pair of horned owls that had become separated began to call to one another. Their hollow, ventriloquial hooting jarred the frosty air, seeming to be deep vibrations rather than a series of notes. Varda moved along her limb, closer to the trunk of the tree to blend into it. She had no knowledge of this morose and powerful killer, the strongest and most courageous of the owls, which does not usually attack the larger raptorial birds unless it is starving, but her instinct was to keep out of its way in the darkness in which it had an overwhelming advantage over her.

THE ADIRONDACKS

THE WEATHER grew warmer toward morning as the wind shifted to the south; ground mist swirled like a ghostly and sluggish sea around the rocks, shrubs, and windfall timber of the opening, and it began to rain. Varda tightened her feathers and sat it out, rousing only momentarily from her hunched and semi-somnolent state when a mink surprised a rabbit, whose despairing screams rang out eerily in the mist below her. She was thoroughly wet when the sun came out at noon, and spent an hour with her wings drooping, her feathers loose and her tail spread out to dry, preening herself afterward and pulling each tail feather through her beak to dress it.

Dry and comfortable once more, she set out again. The spruces laid a shadow on her mind, and she wanted to get away from them. The wind was still against her and she stayed low, flying just above the trees; the miles fell behind her. She was flying so close to the ground and so swiftly that she went through each opening she came to like an arrow. Most of them were barren of life, but in one a dozen blue jays were mobbing a great gray owl, flitting about and screaming in raucous excitement. They were having a splendid time and their attention was concentrated upon their victim, but one of them saw her when she was almost among them and screeched the alarm. They scattered wildly in all directions, but she had already picked one out; she rolled over on her back, swept upward between it and the safety of a spruce, and picked it out of the air.

She plumed and ate it on the topmost branch of a dead tree, and went on. The wind changed in the afternoon and the sun warmed the earth; rising air currents took her high again, and beneath her the country began to change. The massed pines and spruces gave way increasingly to more deciduous trees, their somber greens to the counterpoint of bright gold and crimson. Here and there little farms broke up the woodlands, and narrow roads ran between them.

As the country grew more open and rolling, more stony and barren with the glacial rocks of the Laurentian shield and the concealing, secret spruce forest thinned out, Varda felt more at home; in a measure it resembled the Barrens, where all the vast sweep was open to the sky and the eye could see what moved around on it. She hadn't liked the close growing spruces, hiding everything in their dense and tangled shadows, where prey could only be happened upon accidentally and nothing could be pursued for more than a few feet. It was not her way to hunt in this fashion; it was the realm of the goshawks and the sharpshins, which lurked like cats in the thick growth and made short, swift dashes at their victims. They were supremely maneuverable with their short rounded wings and long tails; they were made for such hunting and she was not. She needed the open, where the eye could see for miles and where speed counted the most and there was room for the long, swift stoop or the headlong, slashing pursuit, where her quarry could not get into thick cover in which her long, narrow wings put her at an overwhelming disadvantage. She would have gone hungry if she had been forced to spend much time in the spruce country, except for luck; another year she would probably remember this and follow the open seacoast.

She went on, flying fast and not inclined to soar and waste time in the pleasure of it; when the wind was against her she dropped low to be shielded from it. She did not consciously know it but she was longing for the sea, the great wide restless plains of the Atlantic and the pale beaches that contained it, and the mysterious intuition that guided her took her toward it. Her lonely way took her down over the farmland and across the wide St. Lawrence between Ottawa and Montreal and into the Adirondacks, that vast state park once haggard from careless lumbering and now preserved and restored, mountainous, covered with forest and filled with glacial lakes. The hardwoods flared in their autumn glory among the pines, and their bright colors dyed the wind-rippled surface of the lakes; the mountains marched off and faded into October haze. The evening caught her and she came down to rest for the night in a high dead tree at the edge of a beaver pond. Chipmunks ran busily about beneath her, filling their storerooms; three deer came quietly to drink and raised their heads together, ears cocked, at a red fox that came to drink as well across the pond from them. The trout in the pond began to dimple the water in their evening rise, and presently the first beaver's head broke the surface as he emerged from his house to set about his night's work. His mate came soon after to join him and they fell to cutting sticks and ferrying them to the vicinity of their house, to sink them to the bottom for winter provender when ice covered their world. The kits of the summer came out last, to swim ashore and play together among the fallen leaves until darkness blotted them out, and far off a barred owl greeted the night.

She was off early the next morning and went hungry, for the forest made poor hunting for her; nearly an hour later, flying strongly, she was a little east of the farm where the bones of John Brown, who hated slavery, had long since gone back into the earth. She could see the bulk of Mt. Marcy to the west, and later dropped down into the trough where Lake George lay and took a bufflehead drake close to the water.

She rested for an hour on an islet of gray rocks and spruces like a dish-garden made by the Japanese and circled high again. The valley of the Hudson River would have been easier, but the shifting winds of mountain flying exhilarated her. She cut through the Appalachians and the rolling Green Mountains at the corner of Vermont, above stone-fenced, hard-won fields and the foundations of farmhouses long abandoned and fallen down and hidden from her by the glow of maples in the sun, the deep old-gold of hickories and pale, gleaming clumps of white birch.

As the land dropped and leveled she saw a red fox running through a long field of rosy-brown grass, mobbed by a great, screaming flock of wheeling crows; in the little calm villages white church steeples stood above the maples and elms. The villages grew closer together and gathered into cities, where factory smoke towered up and flattened and spread long plumes of haze over the land and people went about their concerns below it beside their dirty rivers.

No one saw her except a farm boy who was hunting rabbits after school in the underbrush along the lane of a hilltop farm, and she was upon him and gone before he had time to raise his old single-barreled shotgun, but he retained for a long time a confused impression of her golden coloring shining in the slanting sunlight and her quick, purposeful wingbeats that left him with a feeling of her splendid vitality and power; she seemed to have the stamp of strange and faraway places upon her, for he had never seen her like before. He often thought of her at night in the drowsy time just before he fell asleep and was finally glad, in a half-ashamed way, that he had been unable to shoot her.

The remembrance of him remained with Varda as she traveled, re-enforcing the shadow cast on her mind by the ominous image transmitted through the germ plasm of generations which had encountered man and escaped him, by the memory of similar creatures seen from a distance who had brought the geese dead out of the air at James Bay; his involuntary movement as he turned and half raised the shotgun somehow held more menace than any other animal's approach to attack.

She didn't brood upon the encounter; animals do not forever live with the fear of death; it became part of her education, of her pattern of behavior for the future, which would make her react quickly when the necessity arose. Some creatures never learn this, some have no opportunity, and some learn it incorrectly; they do not usually live very long. Varda was better prepared than these and avoided people. She came over Long Island Sound and crossed it and Long Island itself and Great South Bay to drop on the barrier island well east of Ocean Beach. The beach was lonely and the Atlantic was in front of her, its combers curling green in the autumn sun. She bathed in a small pool of rainwater and dried herself in the cool breeze off the ocean, and for the moment was content.

Two days before, the falconer had left the Arctic by plane. He was anxious to get home in time to meet the peregrine migration on a barrier island off the Maryland coast. For he had been too busy the previous autumn to trap a falcon; he hadn't had one to train for a year; and, like every man who has worked with hawks, handled them and watched them fly, he wanted another. He liked to say that he felt naked without a hawk around, and every time he took a walk in the countryside he missed watching the long wings high above him as the falcon circled over his head waiting for him to flush a bird that it could pursue. It was a companionship unlike any other, in that the man and the essentially wild creature, free but under his control, worked together; the man earthbound but skillful in his management of the bird, the bird free in the boundless air but invisibly bound to and working with the man. There was a fascination in this companionship not found with dogs, horses, or any other domesticated living thing, and seeing Varda golden and curious as she circled the ship had made him long to renew it.

PART II

THE PATHWAY
OF THE SKY

THE ISLAND AND THE MAN

FOR SEVERAL DAYS Varda stayed in this vicinity, to feed and rest. The long trip from James Bay, through a country in which it was difficult for her to take quarry, had reduced a little the reserve fat she had stored up. She was hungry, but feeding well was now no problem. Over fifty species of birds from New England alone crossed Long Island on their migration, and more came from farther north down the coast. Many of the shore birds and herons, early migrants, had already gone through; geese and some early ducks were coming in from the St. Lawrence. Local black ducks were about, and there were lines of cormorants flying low over the sea; Varda took several ducks but most of her quarry were smaller birds: blue jays, sanderlings and flickers, conspicuous, slow-flying, and rather stupid about exposing themselves. There were a number of hawks about:

swift little merlins, ospreys, slow-beating marsh hawks and the active, deadly little sharpshins; there were several young peregrines from the Labrador and Baffin Island coasts, dark birds from the coastal cliffs, which had lived upon sea birds, faced the North Atlantic storms, and seen drift ice from Davis and Hudson Straits. They had come down across the Strait of Belle Isle and the Gulf of St. Lawrence, across Nova Scotia, past the gravelly cliffs of Block Island and over Montauk.

Most of these birds except the peregrines moved west on the Island until they had the shortest water-passage before them. Varda, when she was ready to go, got up on the northeast wind and headed southwest over the sea. She could see no land before her, but that mysterious prescience which man still cannot explain, told her that land was there. An hour later she was in sight of it, and swung down the coast. The wind held and she rode upon it, above the little fishing boats and a distant freighter or two moving across the restless plain of the ocean. Presently she swung past Barnegat light and over the shuttered cottages of Barnegat Island to the Bay. There were many brant on the Bay, trim and lively little geese which bred so far to the north that in ancient times no one knew where they nested and so decided that they hatched from barnacles. They were shy and graceful birds; the blight that had killed the eelgrass, upon which they lived, in the Thirties had nearly done for them. They had managed to switch to other food and survived, but in diminished numbers.

A little farther on she saw a great blue heron flying in the distance, and caught up to him and stooped at him in play. The heron did not know her intentions, but feared them; he vented a white stream of excrement and squawked his apprehension. As she dropped on him like an arrow he turned his head over his back and darted his long beak at her like a rapier, but she ended her stoop a few feet above him, bounded up, and stooped again. This time she slid past close behind him, bounded up and headed him, circled him, made a mock horizontal dash at him and banked vertically away. She was all about him at speed, confusing him with swift and bewildering shifts of maneuver, playing with him, driving him down. She could have killed him easily, but presently she left him crouched protesting on the marsh and took up her way, swinging over to the marshes again along the shore. She missed a kingfisher, which reached the water and dove into it a scant few inches in front of her talons; he popped to the surface and started to fly off, to dive again as she swung back after him. This went on for six shallow stoops, when she tired of it and left him to emerge once more and fly, rattling derisively, to the underbrush ashore.

She had used more energy trying to catch him than he would have returned to her as food. She was hungry now, and a mile down the marsh came hurtling out of the sky again to knock down a young black duck which had forgotten to scan the sky before it took off to join three others that it had seen at a distance. She fed upon it, bathed in a shallow fresh-water pond in the marsh, and dried herself atop an old, leaning stake. The birds of the marsh, knowing in their way that she was hunting no longer, paid no heed to her. As the tide was out the ghost crabs were about their business; she watched them and the birds for an hour before she flew again.

The afternoon was mild and pleasant under a clear sky; beneath Varda the tidal creeks wound about through the marshes that were turning brown, little ponds reflected the sky, and there were a few small boats on the Inland Waterway. It was her humor to fly low, but high above her, taking advantage of the warmed and rising air to soar above man's visual range, a multitude of other hawks were moving south. In the thickets ashore and on the barrier islands the seed eaters were resting and feeding in preparation for their night flights, and restless flocks of them occasionally moved into the open and flew about, where the sunlight winked on their wings as their formations wheeled, and the air over the distant beach was busy with gulls. She flew past a bald eagle perched on a dead tree; his head and tail gleamed white. She had seen few of these great birds on her flight from the Arctic, for their race was sadly diminished.

Gradually the marshes drew in and the Bay narrowed between the mainland and the offshore islands, and the sun sank lower; Varda found a large dry area in the marsh and came down in the middle of it. The gulls strung in to roost around her as the tide came in, noisy in their talk;

shadows lengthened across the marsh, black-capped night herons which once were thought to have a phosphorescent patch on their breasts to attract their prey, came out to feed, and in the gathering darkness the night-flying migrants took to the air and the owls got to their secret work.

Presently the moon came up, round and honey-colored, and as it cleared the earth turned silver, to silver again the sleeping gulls and the drying grasses of the marsh. It shone quietly on a land that was crowded with feathered ghosts, for this land, which had been so changed by man, had once been one of the greatest nesting areas for shore birds and herons on the east coast. Willets, avocets, stilts and bitterns, terns and plover, curlews, oyster catchers, black skimmers and clapper rails had once bred in unbelievable abundance in marshes that were now mostly ditched and drained and dry. The mainland and the island dunes, once the highest along the coast, had been densely forested with hundred-foot oaks, great sassafras, magnolia, sweet gum and holly trees in which vast numbers of great blue, little blue, green and black-crowned night herons and egrets had built their nests. The old trees were gone, replaced by entwined thickets of cedar, holly, and scrub oak, which in their turn had been replaced by bayberry, greenbriar, and weeds; the dunes had been leveled for summer cottages, and the shore birds had been shot out by sportsmen coming from far inland. Many of them had shot a thousand birds or so in a few days. After the shore birds had been decimated or frightened off by spring and fall shooting and their eggs collected by the thousands, attention had turned to the herons, which had been shot in great numbers for their plumage at nesting time.

Belated protection had brought back a scattering of species, but the bird population changed with the change of habitat. It now consisted mostly of grackles, starlings, and robins; what the ornithologists Audubon and Wilson had thought a paradise for birds was now only a point on the route of migration.

The wind had shifted to the south during the night, and there were multitudes of birds in the thickets at Cape May Point waiting for it to change before they took off over the water toward Cape Henlopen when Varda passed there. She didn't see them; flying low and fast into the wind she went down the beach. A few early surf fishermen were out, standing in the spindrift at the edge of the water; most of them didn't know she had gone by. She flew behind them and they were watching their lines, the strings of cormorants farther out, and the few ships on the horizon.

She left the land and crossed Delaware Bay, avoided Rehoboth Beach and made her landfall below it, and swung back over Rehoboth Bay. The sun was higher now and more people, at the shore to enjoy the beautiful October weather, were appearing on the beaches. The Bay was wide and lonely, and more to her taste. Occasionally she passed beneath vees of geese, which had flown all night and were looking for a satisfactory place to come down for a while;

their talk, mellowed by distance, slid past her on the wind.

On the ocean side the shore resorts thinned out; Indian River fell behind her, and the checkered farming country with its pinewoods behind Bethany Beach; Assowoman Bay opened, with the ruled lines of drainage ditches through the bordering marshes. She gained height to pass the Ocean City bridge and came to Sinepuxent Bay and Assateague Island, low and wild, narrow, sandy, and bordered on the Bay side with its marshes and windbeaten pines. She swung toward it. It looked lonely; there were no people within her view; only a single house and a scattered herd of ponies that the Chincoteague Islanders rounded up once a year, drove over to their Island, and sold. It was, in fact, one of the emptiest big barrier islands along the coast. An attempt to develop it had failed, and practically all of the cottages that had been built had broken up and washed away in a great storm several years before.

There was a small ferry crossing the Bay from the mainland with a single Jeep on it, and near the ferry landing another young peregrine was chasing a kingfisher. Varda joined the game for a short time and the two falcons stooped and bounded up into the wind together until the kingfisher lost itself in the marsh grass. The other falcon swung down the Bay shore and Varda hung on the wind for a moment, watching four black skimmers flapping slowly in formation just above the surface of the water, their undershot lower bills picking up small fish. She left them and crossed the belt of pines to the ocean. The waves curled green and broke, smoking with spray, on the deserted beach, and Varda flew several miles down the Island until she came to a wide, flat level that ran from the beach to the Bay and came down. Around her, as far as she could see, the Island seemed as empty of men and their works as the surface of the moon, and nearly as desolate. Several migrating ospreys were in sight and half a mile away, perched on top of a pole, was an old haggard peregrine that paid no attention to her. A few black ducks moved about over the Bay, and gulls flew up and down the beach.

Varda shook herself, and then sat quietly in the sun. Presently a lone Monarch butterfly fluttered past her, close to the sand. This incredible traveler, so small and fragile that it seemed at the mercy of the slightest breeze, would find its way and migrate nearly as far as Varda's course would take her. It had come from the center of the Province of Quebec, and would get nearly to the Gulf of Mexico.

As Varda watched it diminish and disappear across the level the ferry came in to the wharf where the four black skimmers were still flying their formation near the shore, and the Jeep, with two men in it, drove ashore. The man at the wheel was the falconer.

LOST FREEDOM

WITHIN the hour two peregrines flew in from the Bay and came down near a sprawling, half-buried stump a quarter of a mile or so from Varda. One of them was a haggard falcon; the other was a tiercel of the year, one of the haggard's young, who was still following his mother and crying to be fed. He ran around the haggard, wailing and fluttering his wings like a hungry nestling, and although the old bird croaked at him impatiently and moved away from his importunities he followed her and wailed more insistently. Finally she took off into the wind, turned down the beach, and presently came back with a flicker in her foot. He grabbed it from her, turned his back on her, and opening his wings to cover the flicker began to eat it. When he had broken into it and was greedily eating the haggard shuffled off a short distance, took to the air again, and rising steadily disappeared over the Bay. She had borne with him for a long time; now she was finished with him, and he would probably never find her again.

When he had finished the flicker he looked around and was obviously surprised not to see his mother nearby. He looked all about, flew up onto the stump, and wailed several times; then he saw Varda. He flew over to her, and although his crop was bulging he began to wail and flutter his wings at her. Varda gave him a hostile stare, which had no effect; then her feathers stood out in anger and she hissed at him. That had no effect either; she turned from him and he ran around in front of her, still wailing and fluttering. She had had enough; she rose in the air, swung, and bore down upon him. She hit him a thump with her closed foot which rolled him over and over, and flew north up the beach.

Now that she was in the air hunger awoke in her, and she moved back over the bayside tangle of pine and bayberry and greenbriar and flew slowly above it looking for something to pursue. Several flickers and grackles saw her from a distance and dropped into cover. She went on and passed through an opening in the pines where the ruin of an old hotel stood; it had been fifty years since sportsmen had come to it for the shooting, and there wasn't much left of it now. Most of the roof had fallen in, the porches had collapsed, and broken, weathered shingles from its walls littered the sand around it. Shore bird and duck hunters had stayed in it, politicians had hidden there with their women, and furtive bootleggers had used it in the days of Prohibition, but now it had a melancholy air of gaunt decay; the falconer and his companion had driven to it from the ferry and arranged their camping gear in the only sound room that was left. They were driving away from it, out toward the beach, when Varda flew past it.

She continued on, toward the north end of the island, but the two men turned south. They had with them the paraphernalia to catch hawks: a crate of pigeons, a shovel, a wire frame covered with hay that would fit over a man's head and shoulders and look like a clump of grass, which falconers call a headset, several hawk hoods, and three balls of string. The storm that had swept the island had covered it with loose sand; even the road which had been built in the development operation was covered now, and they had to use four-wheel drive most of the time. They drove slowly along, between the dunes and the beach, looking ahead for hawks sitting on the sand. Gulls flapped up and down along the surf, they saw two ospreys, widely separated, and once a bat flitting south. They swung around pieces of driftwood, old, half-buried ships' timbers full of rusted nails, and other flotsam left by the storm; after a few miles they came to the big level where Varda had first come down.

The falconer stopped the Jeep, and hung his binoculars

around his neck. "Look sharp, now," he said to the other man. "Peregrines like to sit on this level; they can see for a long distance all around them."

He started the Jeep again. Half a mile farther on he braked to a sudden stop and put the binoculars to his eyes. "Ah," he said, almost in a whisper, "there's one. Over near that old stump sticking up out of the sand. It's a tiercel, I think. Get me a pigeon out of the crate, please."

His companion got the pigeon for him, and he tied it by one leg to a ball of string. He started the Jeep, drove it four hundred yards down the beach, swung it broadside to the hawk and stopped. "Don't get out on that side," he said. "Get out after me, and cover me up."

He reached behind him and got the shovel and the headset and climbed out of the Jeep on the side away from the bird. He dug a shallow trench and sat down in it facing the hawk, with his legs stretched out. "Put the headset over me, hand me the pigeon, and cover me up," he said. Covered to the sand by what appeared to be a clump of grass, he sat with his hands lying quietly in front of him holding the pigeon. "Drive off about three hundred yards or so and don't get out of the Jeep," he said.

When the Jeep stopped in the distance he threw the pigeon out a little way, let it flutter about, and pulled it back close to the headset again. The distant tiercel, which had been sitting disconsolately since Varda had bowled it over, was still hungry despite the flicker he had eaten; he saw the pigeon at once, and jumped into the air and flew toward it. He approached a foot or two above the sand, but when he got close to the headset he suddenly rose. What birds he had caught for himself when his mother had taken too long to bring in prey had been small ones, and the pigeon looked large. He circled the headset and finally came down on the sand twenty feet away and stood looking at the pigeon. Unconscious of a hidden enemy, his dark eyes on the pigeon, he lowered his head, took two steps, and stopped again. The pigeon was still now, and that further bothered the tiercel who had never seen a bird that wouldn't flee from him. And he had never caught one on the ground. The situation was new to him, and he withdrew a few feet to consider.

Varda flew almost to the inlet at the north end of the island without catching anything, and landed on top of a telephone pole. She sat there for a while, looking about, but there were no birds moving in the vicinity and presently she jumped off the pole and headed back toward the level again. Near the ferry landing she stooped at a grackle, which managed to dive into the greenbriars a scant two inches in front of her talons, and continued on. Soon she had the Jeep in view, but it meant no more to her than a caribou, a pony, or a house. She saw the tiercel sitting on the sand and as she came near it the falconer, in the headset, bumped his pigeon from beneath with his fist to make it move and be more attractive to the tiercel. He didn't see Varda; all his attention was on the tiercel.

The pigeon flapped its wings several times, and Varda caught the movement.

To her it seemed to be caught somehow in a clump of grass, and an easy quarry. She swung instantly, bore down upon the pigeon, and landed upon it. She bit through its neck to kill it, held it firmly through its dying convulsion, shook herself to settle her feathers, and began to plume her quarry. The tiercel, having learned that Varda would not put up with him, flew off.

The falconer, because of his limited view from the headset and because his attention was on the tiercel, hadn't seen her coming. She appeared immediately in front of him so unexpectedly that he barely managed to suppress a great start that would have frightened her off. For a long moment he gloated over her, unsuspecting and golden, busy with the pigeon; then he slowly brought his free hand up and caught her around the legs. Her eight talons with their viselike grip were powerless, and he had her high enough so that she couldn't get her head down to bite him.

For a moment Varda didn't know that she was caught. She felt the hand but ignored it; more than once her quarry had closed its feet around her legs as it died. But the grip tightened, and then the man pushed back the headset with his free hand and heaved himself up out of the sand. He was suddenly immediately in front of her, a great creature who had appeared from nowhere and held her tight; she was shocked and powerless. She spread her wings wide

and beat them to fly away; her eyes burned upon the ap-
parition that had hold of her. The man put his hand on
her; he folded her wings and held them with her legs. The
feathers on her head and neck stood out, she hissed and
tried to bite him; she struggled with all her strength to get
at him but could not. When she saw the hood, she bit at it,
but it was put over her head and blinded her; then a heavy
sock was unrolled down over her body, like a strait jacket,
and thus blinded and bound she was laid on her back on
a seat in the Jeep.

The appalling suddenness with which her world had
changed held her quiet there for a few moments, lost in
kaleidoscopic and shocked impressions, but soon she began
to recover. In the hood it was darker than any night, the
sock pressed in from all sides, and she had never been on
her back before; all of these things were intolerable to her
spirit and her pride, and filled her not with fear but with
rage. She began to fight against them, hissing and rolling
about in the sock; she felt the Jeep start off and she continued her struggles as it bumped noisily along and bounced
her around on the seat.

Back at the old hotel where the falconer was stopping
she was handled again. The sock was rolled off her, and
leather straps were put on her legs. These jesses each had
a slit in the free end so that they could be fastened through
a double-eyed swivel, and a six-foot leather leash was run
through the swivel's other eye. The swivel turned and
prevented the leash and jesses from tangling as the hawk

moved about. This tackle, which had come down from
the earliest days of falconry, was so effective that it had
been changed very little in over two thousand years. After
the leather was on, Varda was placed on a horizontal perch
made from a two-by-four with an old blanket draped over
it, and left to sit for a while to compose herself.

She sat in the darkness of the hood, gripping the perch.
Being off her back and free of the confining sock she felt
better; the hood was tight around her neck and she
scratched at it to get it off, but it remained secure. Several
times she ruffled her feathers to settle the disarray that the
man's hand and the sock had caused, and hearing the noises
around her as the men prepared their dinner and ate it she
hissed at them. Violence had been done her; she didn't
know where she was or what else threatened; she sat up
straight and moved her head to follow the sounds, ready for
defiance or defense in the dark.

The sounds went on for a considerable time; when it
grew dark her captor lit a candle, got the pigeon that Varda
had killed and pulled a wing and a breast off it; he put on
his falconer's glove and laid the pigeon breast in it. He
walked to the perch, put the gloved hand behind Varda,
made a fist, and pressed against the back of her legs. Her
balance was disturbed and the glove was alien; she gripped
the perch harder and hissed, opening her wings. The glove
pressed harder, so that in the end she had to step back-
wards on it or fall blind into the darkness. The man put
the jesses through his fingers, sat down with his back to

the wall, struck the hood laces with his teeth and free hand, and slipped the hood off.

Varda could see now; in the dim light, with the flickering candle casting wavering black shadows around the walls, she was in a new and alien world, confined and facing two of the creatures she had learned to avoid. The wide sky and its safety were gone; the men were staring at her. In her world a stare was a preliminary to attack, and for a moment she was prepared to withstand it; her feathers stood out, her eyes burned with fury, and she hissed at them. She needed room and freedom, and jumped off the gloved fist to regain them. The jesses jerked at her legs and held her; she was brought up sharply, and hung head down from the hand and futilely beat her wings. A hand came up under her and tossed her back upon the fist again, and she hissed and bit at it and immediately jumped off once more. The hand put her back; it continued to put her back, dispassionately and tirelessly, until her breath was gone and she stood panting and hot, with her wings drooped.

She didn't fear the hand; she hated it. It was an offense against her dignity. When it moved she hissed at it and her feathers stood out in menace; when it came near she bit savagely at it. It moved about, it was never still; once she was quicker than the hand and got her beak into it, and the blood flowed. But the hand came back; it moved the meat in the glove, and she bit into the meat and pulled it out of the glove and cast it from her.

It was put back, and she cast it away once more. It was put back again and again, gently but inexorably, and she cast it away and jumped off the glove and hung ignominiously from it, to be put back again and again.

This went on for two hours, while the shadows cast by the flickering candle danced wildly around the walls. Varda grew tired; her muscles ached from jumping against the jesses, which always pulled her up with a jarring wrench, and her throat and lungs grew dry from her continuous defiant hissing. She was unbeaten, but she was not stupid. She realized, wearily and at last, that she couldn't get away or prevail and that the man hadn't done her any real harm, and so she quieted. His movements had been calm, not abrupt or threatening, and after his first stare he had been careful to avert his glance from her when he could. Being young, she was more malleable than a haggard, which would have continued to fight. Her spirit wasn't broken; it would never be; she simply had come to the realization that the thing which had happened to her had to be endured. She was spent and hungry, and the glove held meat. She leaned over quickly and tore at it, and swallowed a piece. She watched the man and hissed warningly at him, but he sat quietly and made no hostile move.

She took another bite, and another. Several times the man moved a little to rearrange the meat so that she could get at it more easily, until she realized that he was helping her and allowed it. When the meat was gone he quietly hooded her and tied her on the perch to sleep. He was well satisfied with her, for she was clever; he had seen many birds which had fought for a week or more and refused to eat except clumsily, with the hood on, but she had quickly realized her condition, accepted it, and made the best of it.

He watched her for a few minutes and as he watched she fell asleep. Her head, heavy with the unaccustomed hood on it, dropped down to hang in front of her breast. Perhaps she knew that the first link in the chain of her captivity had been forged and that for a while the wide sky would bear her up no more; occasionally, threatened in dreams by the haunting shadows of the remembered and disastrous day, she would rouse uneasily and hiss defiance at them and fall asleep again.

THE LURE

VARDA had awakened early all of her life and watched the
light of day strengthen over the world, but the next morning there was no light; she knew the dawn had come, but
she couldn't see it. She moved restlessly, stretched one
wing and then the other, and scratched at the hood which
held her blinded on the perch. Presently the men awoke
and the sounds of their moving about began. They ate
breakfast and packed up, for now that the falconer had
his hawk he was going home. Varda was picked up on the
fist again; the perch was moved into the back of the Jeep
and she was taken out and put upon it and tied down.

She could feel the sweet coolness of the early morning
air after the stuffy room and hear the distant grumbling
of the surf; she half spread her wings in longing, and then
folded them again. The engine of the Jeep started and

the jolting, noisy, interminable ride began. She was pre-occupied with maintaining her balance as the Jeep bounced, slithered, started, and stopped. The ferry crossing was the only good part of the trip, and it was soon over; once on the mainland the ride was smoother but the noise began again. It built up along her nerves; presently she could stand it no more, preferring to fall in darkness, and jumped from the perch in spite of the hood. The jesses pulled her up and she hung head down, beating her wings against the camping gear.

The Jeep stopped and the sock was rolled down over her once more. She made the rest of the trip in it; several hours later, when noise and motion had ceased, she was taken out of the sock and put on a hawk block in a quiet yard.

Later she was taken on the fist again, the man walked around, became still, and her hood was taken off. Now she was in a different room, which held more light. The man was sitting down and she was very close to him; a blue ticked setter lay quietly on the floor. She had been cut off in a world of darkness and uproar, and stuffed into a sock; she had been confined and jounced about; outraged and surrounded by these new alien things she forgot the night before. She sat very still for a second or two; then she jumped sideways from the man's fist, spreading her wings to fly away. The jesses stopped her with a jerk and she hung head down, beating her wings futilely as before, and as before the hand came up under her back and re-turned her to the fist.

As she had hated it before as an affront to her dignity, she hated it now; but despite her overwhelming desire to escape she began to remember how inexorable the hand had been and the futility of trying to escape it. She didn't jump again; but she hissed in defiance, the feathers on her head stood out in menace, and her dark eyes stared down at the man. The setter rolled her eyes up at Varda and her tail thumped several times in good will on the floor, and Varda hissed at her. The man carried her into the dining room and sat down at the table to eat, for the constant movement of eating is very helpful in showing a hawk that motion is not hostile. At first every time his hand moved Varda hissed at it; she hissed at everything. Gradually she came to see the uselessness of it and to remember that she had not been harmed the night before, and ceased.

At the end of dinner she was carried into the living room again. The man sat down and smoked a pipe, holding Varda as he read quietly for an hour. She watched him, ready for defiance but calmer now; she was trying to fathom him. He was a large and potentially dangerous animal but he had not been hostile; he had hold of her but he had made no motion of attack; there was almost a quizzical expression in her eyes as she steadily regarded him. He had even fed her, and presently he fed her once more. This time she ate with less delay, watching him meanwhile. Presently he smoked again, and as the smoke eddied about it puzzled her and she watched it. It was a new and strange thing, and piqued her curiosity enough so that she removed her attention from him for short periods of time, cocking her head until it was almost upside down to follow the slow, mysterious swirling of the smoke.

In the quiet of the room there was still no hostile motion and, besides, there were interesting things to see. She remained wary but could find nothing that actually threatened her, and so made a small beginning toward accepting the man and the dog. Later, when the man stroked her lightly a few times with a pigeon wing feather as a start toward accustoming her to being touched, she drew her head back and opened her beak slightly in warning but accepted the stroking. She had been touched with feathers in the eyrie, by her brothers, her sister, and her parents; presently she would accept the hand. Close to midnight he hooded her and took her out to the little hawk house beside the garage and tied her on the perch for the night. He left her hooded; bareheaded she would probably jump off at first light and hang by her jesses. Hawk perches have canvas or some similar material hanging from them, so that if a hawk jumps off and is pulled up by its jesses it can turn and claw its way back up again. Varda didn't yet know how to do this; she would have to learn, while the man was there to help her, and until she did learn the hood would be kept on her while she was on the perch.

The days went on, and as every action of the man was pointed toward convincing her of his good intentions she gradually lost her distrust and came to accept him; her wild defiance disappeared. She was carried for hours and became accustomed to the proximity and actions of the man and the places he took her. She was always fed on the fist; and as trained hawks are controlled by their appetite, and the meat given her was carefully controlled in amount to leave her unsatisfied, she was always hungry and looking forward to the meat-garnished glove.

She who had always fed herself bountifully became a pensioner, and as her manning went on she was made a little hungrier all the time. She lost weight, the roundness of her breast fell away and her keel grew sharp, and her residual fat was used up. What remained of her instinct to avoid men became subordinated to her hunger. She had accepted the proximity of her former enemy; now she had to do even more, and come to him instead of moving away from him as her deepest instinct told her to do. First she was made to step to the fist to be fed, and then to fly increasing distances to it. She was introduced to the lure, a small pillow-shape of leather with meat tied upon it, and when she knew it, she was taken outdoors to be flown to it on a string.

When the lure was thrown, Varda bobbed her head and opened her wings, drawn by hunger and the habit of feeding on the lure, then checked herself; she remembered the many times the jesses had jerked her back. The man dropped his fist a little, and rolled it, and she was in the air. She righted herself and flew toward the lure.

It was the first time she had truly flown since her capture, the first time, unimpeded, that she had had the air under her wings. A great joy went through her. The lure and its meat drew her strongly but the wide and windy sky, with its freedom and its pleasures, its memories of happy wanderings and wild games with the gales and roaring headlong stoops at living quarry drew her more strongly still. She came to the lure and made her choice and rose over it, heading upward.

The man carefully tightened his fingers on the string that was tied to her swivel, stopping her and bringing her down. She landed clumsily, with her eyes still on the far horizon, and stood confused. Before she realized that she was still captive she tried several more times to jump into the air and fly away, but the string held her. Finally she uttered a creaking protest, low and wistful, and then gave up her attempts and walked over to the lure. She was not hungry enough yet.

ESCAPE

BETWEEN the times that she was carried on the glove, Varda was now put out on a block in the daytime to "weather," as falconers say. At least she was in the sun and the open air once more. There was a leash of leather four feet long on her and she could bathe in a small tub of water, walk around the block, and jump down from it and up onto it again. She had a long view over the countryside, across several fields and a stream and a rising, wooded hill beyond it. She could watch the winter birds that flitted around in the shrubbery; juncos, chickadees, a pair of cardinals and several tree sparrows that had come from near

her eyrie on the Barrens. Several flocks of crows on their flight line to and from their roost passed not far off in the mornings and afternoons and cawed at her; a wintering kestrel, a bright little male, occasionally appeared and took a few stoops at her, crying his *killy-killy-killy;* once or twice a wintering redtail, seeing her on the block, would land in a tree not far off and watch her for a while. Few of them would have come so close if they hadn't known she was tied. At first she tried to fly off, but as the leash always pulled her up she soon learned its limit and stopped jumping against it.

Her food was cut down a little more, and she was flown at the lure daily on the string. At first she tried several more times to rise over the lure and be free, but the string always held her; and so there came to be built up in her mind, between her hunger and the string, a conviction that she was somehow attached to the lure. When this conviction became strong enough and sufficiently impressed to make her reaction practically certain, the man decided that the day had come to fly her free. This is the day that makes the falconer nervous; he has no certain hold on his bird. Some unexpected thing may happen to frighten her badly enough so that she will forget her training and go off, and all of his hopes and patient hard work will have gone for nothing.

He put bells engraved with his name and address on her so that he could find her if she came down in high grass or underbrush, and picked a day when there was no wind to buoy her up and tempt her to ride upon it. The setter was left in the house, although Varda had long since accepted her. She had also accepted other people, cars, and practically everything that she would ever see in her captivity, but her trainer was taking no chances.

He put her on the block, took the leash and swivel off her, and walked away from her for a hundred feet. He had two falconry bags over his shoulders, one of which held the lure well garnished with meat; the other held a live pigeon on a long string. He stopped and faced her, took the lure out, swung it around his head and threw it from him. Varda was very hungry; she had not been fed the night before; she flew directly to the lure and began to eat, and the man breathed a sigh of relief, carefully took her up, and finished feeding her on his fist.

The next day she was kept in the air a little longer. The lure was pulled away from her so that she had to circle and return to it. Every day thereafter her flying time was extended a little; she was allowed to go farther away and get higher into the air, and her daily ration was increased to strengthen her.

A better time began for her now, for she was flying again. Her muscles were stiff from long inactivity, but all the remembered keen pleasure of flight was hers once more, and as her muscle tone improved with exercise her pleasure increased. When she moved too far away the lure was shown her, to bring her back. Presently, when she was high above him, the man gave a yell and threw out a live pigeon for her. The fierce joy of pursuit, which she hadn't known for so long, awoke in her like a sudden wild flame and she rolled over and stooped; the air roared past her as she plummeted down. She came so fast that the pigeon dodged too late. Her closed foot hit it a stunning blow and it fell, streaming feathers. Varda turned and shot upward until her momentum was gone and then spiraled swiftly down to grasp it in her foot. She broke its neck and held it, looked around, and gave two sharp croaks of satisfaction. She was allowed to eat all of it, to impress upon her the desirability of working with the man.

Another pigeon was thrown out beneath her in a day or so, and she began to watch for them. She kept a sharper eye upon the man. She circled high over his head, waiting, a maneuver that falconers call *waiting on*. Presently he began to take the setter with him, to train Varda for game hawking. He put a pigeon's head under its wing, held it with both hands, swung it in a circle, and hid it in the grass. The circular swinging confused the pigeon and it lay quietly until the dog found and pointed it and the man flushed it; then Varda made her stoop. From this Varda quickly learned to keep her eye on both dog and man. When the setter stopped in her hunting and stiffened to a point, Varda, if she had waited on too long and drifted off, would quickly be back overhead again.

She was now taken hunting, carried on the fist until the setter found a lark or a pheasant and made a point, and then cast into the air. Seeing the setter on point, she would swiftly ring up until she was high overhead. Once she had her pitch she would hold her circle, expectantly, until the game was flushed; then she would roll over, give a few rapid wingbeats to increase her speed, and come down like a meteor to strike.

This was the thing that falconers love to see: the impetuous plunge, swift as a falling star, so breath-taking and seemingly so reckless but in reality so perfectly controlled. Varda liked to wait on very high for it gave her command of a wider area, and her stoop was a long one, extremely fast; often she would beat her wings most of the way down to increase her speed. She was kinder than the shotgun, for she never wounded her quarry so that it would go off and die slowly; she either killed it cleanly or missed it altogether and it escaped unscathed into cover.

The falconer had never had a better hawk, and rejoiced in her. She was beautiful to look at, golden, burnished, with a perfect mail of hard feathers and a dignity and presence to go with her appearance; a pleasure to handle, calm and even-tempered, unparalleled in the air among the falcons he had trained. As for Varda, she keenly enjoyed the game. She could have been in worse case; she could have fallen into the hands of someone who would have starved or mistreated her, or let her sit on the block for months, eating her heart out. For a captive, she was fortunate; she had fallen into good hands, but she was still a captive. She was flown and brought down and leashed to her block to watch the little birds in the yard around her go free. The freedom she had been born for, the wide wandering and the limitless sky, had been taken away from her and even in her freest moments she was bound by an invisible cord to the lure.

There came a windy, bright winter morning. Varda, on her block, saw the falconer approaching and she spread her wings; she wanted to fly. The man's eyes lighted up at the sight of her, so eager and golden in the sun. The wind, which had been stronger than he liked all day, had now picked up a little more; it was a wind that a falcon might drift off upon, but he decided to fly her anyhow. He went into the house for his windbreaker and walking shoes. He put his falconry bags over his shoulders, whistled up the setter, took Varda from her block, and started out.

They were nearly a mile from home, near a small field of corn that had been left standing, when the dog came to a point at the edge of an acre of waist-high brush. The man took Varda's leash and swivel off, and cast her into the air. She went off in a wide circle, rising quickly on the wind, and took a lofty pitch; almost a thousand feet above him she came into the wind and hung nearly motionless.

On the ground the dog began to show indecision; she broke her point and cast a few feet back and forth. The pheasant had moved, and the wind flawed the scent. The falconer ran in but the pheasant wasn't there; it had crept into the cornfield, and the dog found the line and went after it. The man cursed and followed. The pheasant would be difficult to flush, with the falcon hanging over it like Nemesis and the cornfield to run about and hide in. The falconer had a fleeting thought that he should bring Varda down with the lure and move on. The wind was half a gale; but he was so confident of her by now, so sure that she would stay over him, that he didn't do it. Because the cornfield wasn't very large he thought that he and his dog would soon have the pheasant up, and he concentrated his efforts on that.

Varda hung motionless for a moment after the setter disappeared, and then swung a little. She could see the man's head and shoulders above the brown cornstalks and watched him a little longer from her widening circle, but the wind tempted her; it had been a long time since she had been able to play upon such a wind. The remembered delight of tumbling about on it, of swooping down and being carried effortlessly and wildly up, awoke in her. She drifted farther off, rolling and free as an autumn leaf on the gale, high above the long hills with their marching companies of bare and wintry trees, the long brown fields, and the green patches of winter wheat.

It was then that a wintering mallard drake, which that morning had pitched into the creek behind the house, decided to move to the river a few miles away. He jumped into the air, and although no man could have seen him at that distance, Varda saw him immediately. He was better to eat than a pigeon and easier to catch, a direct flyer without the capability for quick, evasive shifts, and the pursuit of ducks had been part of her freedom. She went after him at once.

Angling down on the wind from her high pitch, she picked up speed rapidly; her long wings sang on the air. The drake had a mile start of her, but she drew in on him swiftly; he saw her and put on his best speed, quacking with alarm. The chase was a long one and her wind hadn't been much improved by the comparatively small amount of flying that she had been doing in her captivity, but in sight of the river she caught him and brought him down.

She fed on him fully, having been kept lean and hungry for so long. Then she flew to the river, bathed at the edge of it, and dried herself in the sun. An hour later she flew five miles farther down the river and perched in a tall, pale-mottled sycamore for the night.

THE GAUNTLET

WHEN trained falcons get away, or catch something out of sight of the falconer and feed upon it, they more often than not return to the locality where they have been flown for a time and stay in that locality for several days. It has become in a sense their territory, and draws them back; many times the man who has been flying them can pick them up again within a day or two.

The inclination to return to the familiar vicinity of the falconer's house was in Varda's mind when she awoke high in the sycamore the next morning, but several things weakened it. The overcast sky took on wide streaks of color in the east and promised bad weather, and there was a skim of ice, fragile and silvery, along the edges of the river. A hundred yards away, back from the shore, a belated raccoon which had ranged far that night climbed a gray beech and distracted her. He turned his little black highwayman's mask this way and that to give his world a final glance, and disappeared into his hollow to sleep. He knew that a storm was coming and had fed well to wait it out. The north wind brought the same message to Varda. She should feed again before the coming storm made it difficult; also she wanted to satisfy the desire, which had never altogether left her, for the south.

These inclinations were almost on balance and she might have returned if she hadn't seen a kingfisher flying farther down the river. She dropped from the sycamore and went after it. It gave its rattling cry and fled before her, bright blue against the cold, leaden color of the river, dropped as she got close to it, and disappeared with a splash into the water. She left it, and flew on; presently she rounded a sharp bend in the river and came upon an old gray stone barn over which a flock of pigeons were wheeling. As she put on speed all except one of them saw her and dropped quickly to scramble through the opening between the barn wall and the eaves. The single remaining pigeon was sick; it was dying of a parasite named *Trichomonas*, and it wasn't so alert as the others. It saw her belatedly and dropped for the opening. Varda swerved and rolled sideways; she flashed past it, her rear talon raked a few feathers from it, but it got into the barn. She was fortunate that she hadn't caught it, for the infection she would have got from eating it would have killed her in a week, ruining her liver and closing up her throat.

Thinking that she had knocked the pigeon down, Varda banked a tight half circle and returned, flying along the barn wall to search the ground. The pigeon wasn't there, and this puzzled her; she swung up and perched on the ridge of the barn roof, which she would never have done before she was manned. The farmer, having finished his breakfast, had been standing at his living room window, which faced the barn; he had seen the flurry among his pigeons, and he saw Varda land on the roof. He ran to get his shotgun, but it was not in its accustomed place; by the time he found it Varda had given the pigeon up and taken to the air again. She had narrowly escaped death twice within five minutes.

She would continue to escape it now only if fortune continued to favor her, for the falconer had taken her natural wariness of man away when he manned her. She had accepted and worked with him, and to her inexperience he represented all men. If he had purposely set her free he would have done it in wild and empty country where she would have had a chance to forget his proximity and the routines of training, and gradually regain her wariness. Now, stripped of her defense, she would have to travel a populous country where most men's hands would be against her.

Half an hour later she escaped death again. She was flying low and fast over a large cornfield in which a man was hunting rabbits with a beagle. The field had been harvested with a mechanical cornpicker, which had left windrows of dried stalks on the ground, and a pigeon that had been feeding among them rose immediately in front of her. She caught it by a quick swerve and came down to plume and eat it. It had all happened so quickly that the man, who was not far off but was looking the other way at the time, didn't see her. He passed within forty yards, not hearing her bells as she fed because the earflaps on his cap were down and not seeing her between the windrows. The beagle heard her bells and ran over to investigate. He looked at her, bright-eyed, from a distance of ten yards or so and then went off busily on his hunting, wagging his tail. Birds were no concern of his; his master was a chicken raiser, and he had spent his life among them.

Presently she went on again, flying higher now that she had fed, over the flat, dun country patched with woodland and farms; by the middle of the day she had crossed the broad mouth of the Susquehanna, where it empties into the head of Chesapeake Bay. There were rafts of ducks resting quietly. She was back to broad water again, the land of innumerable bayside marshes, winding slow rivers and tidal creeks, of sandy soil, mistletoe green in the oaks and holly trees growing more frequently in the woods.

A circling plane was testing bombs over Aberdeen Proving Grounds, and the regular, jarring concussions sent her over to the Bay's eastern shore. Within the hour she flew over the Bay bridge, and when well past it came down to rest for an hour, for her limited flying had lowered her condition a little.

She had dropped a little below the area of the storm, which would only touch this country with its edge as it turned northeast; there was intermittent sunshine, and it was pleasant to sit in the sun. From her dead tree in the marsh, which held an old, decaying osprey's nest, she could see a few muskrat houses, a marsh hawk beating back and forth, and several turkey vultures lazily soaring in the distance. A few crows moved about, giving her a wide berth, and a kestrel flew past and took a playful stoop at her. Within the hour a wind came up and gradually increased, bringing a drop in temperature with it. The dried marsh grass bowed in running waves before it, and a loose stick in the old nest below Varda began a melancholy ticking as it swung to and fro. The quiet and the drowsy, peaceful warmth were gone, and she took to the air again.

Although it was not a soaring day any longer she still wanted to be high; perhaps her new freedom, the opportunity to sit in the sun as long as she wished or move about, had something to do with it. She was rested now and began to play a little on the wind, rising up as she went. She drifted across the land below Cambridge, and presently, as she crossed the big flat fields, saw a man hunting quail with a dog. The habit of waiting on over the falconer's setter was still strong in her; she flew toward them, swung into the wind, and took her pitch high over the quartering dog.

Soon it came to a point. The man walked in, the covey flushed, and Varda started down. The man shot twice, and two quail crumpled. Varda had been so high that she was still in her stoop as the quail started to fall. The shots jarring the air and the tumbling quail brought back to her in a flash the shot geese at James Bay. If it hadn't been for that early and profound impression she would probably have landed on one of the fallen quail or struck a live one and come down on it; because of this experience her response to the situation beneath her was to avoid it and get away. She swerved, pulled out of her stoop among the floating quail feathers, and scudded past the man who stood astonished with an empty gun.

She quickly gained height again, and turned back over the Bay. She had passed over rafts of ducks on the water in the morning, and as she went on saw an increasing number of them in the air; the rising wind made them restless, and they began to wander about. There would nearly always be ducks somewhere within her view from now on; she had come to the wintering ground that had drawn them from the Bear River marshes of Utah's Great Salt Lake to the northernmost islands of the Arctic Ocean and the top of Greenland. Most of the rafted ducks, resting in deep water, were divers: redheads, canvasbacks, and scaup. They had come east, across the migration routes of most birds, from the prairie country where they had raised their broods in potholes and on little lakes. They had formerly existed in much greater numbers; now they were in trouble. More esteemed for the table than most of the others, they had been mercilessly shot by market hunters and sportsmen for many years; a great many of their breeding places had been drained for use as farmland in a country that already had a problem of surplus crops, and several years of drought had further reduced their numbers by drying up many of the remaining potholes before the young could fly.

The others, mallards, blacks, ruddys, pintails, widgeon and baldpates, were surface feeders, pond and river ducks; they stayed near shore, or in the creeks. They were also reduced but in better case; their breeding places had been let largely alone, and being mostly in ponds and little tributary creeks hadn't suffered the effects of the pollution with which men had filled the rivers.

Varda saw them all; a great wealth of ducks was scattered beneath her as she traveled down the eastern shore of the Bay; there were also innumerable blinds from which to shoot them. Many a farmer made more money by renting his waterfront land to duck hunters than he did from working his farm, and most of the cornfields had goose pits in them, surrounded by decoys.

As the gray afternoon wore on the birds that had been resting through the middle of the day began to take to the air in their thousands, moving out to feed. Long lines of

geese strung their skeins high across the sky, talking together, circling the cornfields of their intention, side-slipping down; canvasbacks and redheads got up for their
afternoon exercise flights, moving fast and high, an occasional slanting shaft of sunlight winking on their wings, and
the river ducks in their swiftly moving flocks swung into
feeding locations, grew suspicious, and swung away again
like ghosts on the wind to seek other places. Many hunters,
taking a chance with the law, baited the water around their
blinds with corn, and the ducks sought it. As sunset approached it was impossible to look in any quarter of the
sky and not see waterfowl etched somewhere against it, and
gunfire rolled around the compass.

Varda was well down the Bay, and it was nearly time to
perch for the night. She was very high and a small flock
of scaup crossed under her as she was over a little river
emptying into the Bay. They drew together compactly as
they saw her. Most peregrines will not stoop at a tight
flock of ducks, preferring singles or a loose bunch from
which they can pick one out, but she rolled over and
stooped at them. They dropped in a body, side-slipping,
each with one wing folded; the air roared through the
canted primaries of their single opened wings. Two men in
a blind below looked up, startled by the sound. They saw
her close the flock like a meteor, merge with it, and pick
up a duck at the edge of the bunch. As she scudded by
them with the duck in her talons they both shot at her, but
she was going so fast that they didn't lead her enough; they

were ten feet behind her, and she went on into the marsh near shore to come down.

After she had fed on the scaup she flew up into an oak to perch. There was a meandering creek almost under her and presently, at the edge of twilight, a boy who had a string of muskrat traps along the creek came by. He was carrying a stick and three dead muskrats; Varda moved when she saw him, and he heard the sound of her bells. He looked up at her, wondering what manner of bird she could be, wearing bells and looking so calmly down at him.

"Shoo!" he said, waving his stick and wishing that he had brought his gun. He usually had it with him, for occasionally he found a duck or a goose with a broken wing along the creek and shot it, but he had loaned the gun to a friend that morning.

"Shoo!" he said again.

Varda didn't move and the boy finally went on, to get to the end of his trapline before dark.

HATTERAS

THE STORM to the north had turned northeast early in the
night; the fringe of it had left a light dusting of snow, but
the morning dawned calm and clear. The small birds began
to move about and a deer, pursued by four hounds that had
been out all night, ran through the marshes not far from

Varda's tree and swam the little river to get away from them. Presently a flock of swans crossed the river, between her and the Bay; the colors of sunrise dyed faintly their white feathers, and their talk sounded like a distant pack of beagles trailing. Skeins of geese moved over the falcon, and the early morning flights of redheads and canvasbacks; as the sun's rim cleared the horizon the guns began again.

Varda sat on; she was in no hurry to get into the air. After the broken clouds and cold wind of yesterday afternoon and more flying than she had had in months she found pleasure in the feel of the early sun, and she hadn't cast. The feathers she had eaten as she fed the night before were still in her crop and after a bit she regurgitated them, rolled up tight in the shape of a cocoon. A mallard hen swam around the head of the reach of the creek, saw her, and turned back around the corner again. It was sick of lead poisoning, and had come into the marsh to die. There were twenty-six shotgun pellets in its gizzard, picked up from the bottom with bait corn in front of a blind; six pellets would have been enough to kill it. Many less than the mallard carried had brought lingering death to innumerable ducks. Varda dropped from her tree and cut across the marsh to make a shallow stoop at it, but it still had sufficient strength to dive and swim under water and avoid her.

She went on, caught a blackbird and ate it, bathed, dried herself for an hour, and circled widely until she found an updraft from the warming earth to ride into the sky. There being little wind, the morning flight of ducks was over early; it was going to be what the duck hunters call a bluebird day, when ducks sleep in the sun and feed late.

At two thousand feet she found a little wind behind her and traveled with it, soaring with her tail spread, in long ellipses in the cool and sunny air; the great and silent pleasure of soaring was hers once more, and for miles the Bay and the labyrinthine twistings of its shoreline spread out below her.

The rich meat of her recent feedings and her new-found freedom were already bringing her back into high condition again; she saw a distant marsh hawk patrolling his beat a few feet above the marsh, took a long, wild stoop at him in play, and bounded up to her pitch again. She also saw many duck hunters, for they were bored with their quiet day and moved about carelessly in their blinds or near them. She saw several of them drop two restless ducks and move out to pick them up, and the incident joined in her consciousness that shadowy, warning recollection that had saved her from the quail hunter. She was still close to the falconer's manning, but these things were rapidly moving her away from the effects of it. As the long hunger which had been the keystone of that manning grew satisfied, and as she moved into the emptier reaches of the winter coast, she would see fewer men and tend to avoid them more. She still needed luck, and so far she had had it.

Caught up in the pleasure of soaring she moved with comparative slowness down the Bay, making a little easting toward the lower end of Pocomoke Sound. She had passed the mouth of the Potomac, muddy and opaque with the topsoil and wastes that it was bringing down; opposite the Rappahannock's mouth she was over the shoreline again, and from her pitch could see, hazy in the distance, the Atlantic and the many bays and barrier islands along the ocean shore. The far white line of the surf drew her; she changed course and crossed the peninsula, dropped down, and began to fly again.

The lonely and isolated clutter of coastal islands, desolate but enlivened with gulls and sea ducks, fell behind her one by one; the winter Atlantic grumbled and tossed its white spray into the wind and scoured the pale beaches. The quick little sandpipers played tag with the waves, their legs twinkling, and on a lonely small island not far above Cape Charles lighthouse she struck two of them down, ate them, and perched for the night on a wooden box which had once held Scotch whisky that the sea had left on the crest of the beach. There was a bank of clouds to the west; the sun went down, dyeing them to a fiery splendor that slowly paled to a delicate dusty rose until the coming night leached them of all color, and the stars came out. A hungry fox from the shoreside thickets, working the beach for whatever crumbs the sea tossed him, caught Varda's scent, moved discreetly around her, and trotted on.

The day dawned fine, with a high, thin drift of clouds and a mild wind from the north; Varda awoke with a great sense of well-being. It was one of those rare, high winter days when men drop if they can the concerns that hold them and sit bemused and grateful in the cool breeze and the sun, thinking, if they think at all, of the mellow, golden time of October or the opening buds of spring. Perhaps Varda, so far from the bleak sweep of the Barrens now, had an intimation of the south: warmth and the sun, live oaks with their ghostlike veils of Spanish moss, beaches backed by palmettos standing above the thickets, marshy sea islands; the mangrove thickets, the teeming, exuberant life of the land and the sea, the lovely clear water of the Keys shading from purple to aquamarine and breaking on the beaches in gleaming spray. The Keys were where the tiercel, her father, had come from in the spring, and that mysterious corner of her brain which guided her, a legacy from him, waited to recognize them and signal her down.

A school of dolphins went by beyond the breakers, playing happily as they rose to breathe and curve downward into the green water again; she watched them until they passed and took to the air. She hadn't cast and wasn't very hungry; in any event, her bent for the south now was greater than her appetite. She spent no time in hunting and flew swiftly, straight and low, rising a little after she passed the lighthouse, to be above the ships moving in and out of the Bay.

The long waves crawled beneath her, with a running glitter of sun on them. She flew over a tanker on its way to Baltimore; a few miles to the west of her, a hundred years past, the guns of *Monitor* and *Merrimac* had echoed over the water to bring to an end the days of tall sailing ships and usher in a change in the world.

A flight of canvasbacks, strong flyers, the drakes gleaming in the sun, passed below her a few feet above the waves. The day's first real hunger stirred in her; she broke her rhythm, swung to stoop and decided against it, and straightened for the south again. She passed Cape Henry and presently was off the barrier beach seaward of Currituck Sound, long beloved by duck hunters; a few miles below the Virginia line, north of Kitty Hawk, hunger brought her in to take an oyster catcher and feed upon it. She was coming into the area now where many shore birds wintered and the low plain of the coast, full of marshes and swamps and wandering tidal creeks, became even flatter and more full of water. The Great Dismal Swamp, that large and trackless place where a man could lose himself among the featureless waterways, where bears, wild turkeys, otters and other creatures sometimes spent all their lives without seeing mankind, lay to the west of her beyond the Sound. There had been several schemes to drain it and they had come to nothing; it had escaped progress, and in its innermost, gloomy, tangled reaches still held its secrets.

Varda saw none of this. She rested for a while and went on down the open barrier beach, passed Kitty Hawk with its high dunes and the monument to the two brothers who had, for good or ill, showed men the way into the air.

The Outer Banks and Hatteras lay before her, the narrow strip of sand running triangularly out into the sea that has drowned so many men and broken the backs of so many ships. Fogs and sudden, unexpected storms haunt it, for it is the dividing line where the cold currents of the ocean, coming from as far north as Davis Strait, meet the warm upper layers of the Gulf Stream coming north from the tip of Florida. The disparate currents and the air masses they bring with them clash like two marching armies at this line which more truly divides the north and the south than any arbitrary one fixed by men, bringing bad weather and in their turbulent opposing forces throwing up the ridge that is the Outer Banks on the shallow submarine shelf off the coast.

It is the gathering place of great schools of dolphins and southern fishes hungry for oily prey from the cold vitamin-rich waters of the north, and for myriads of birds escaping the hunger and iron frosts of their nesting grounds. As Varda crossed high over the Bodie Island lighthouse and Oregon Inlet and came above Pea Island Refuge she could see scattered about in the distance on Pamlico Sound the white flocks of greater snow geese and big whistling swans, Canada geese and ducks. Pea Island was a protected area, one of the great chain of refuges set aside by the Fish & Wildlife Service on the migration flyways of the nation where birds could rest and feed in safety and peace. Most of the birds on it went no farther south; the snow geese were the most numerous for they liked the vicinity of Pea Island, and the greater part of their entire population ended its migration here; the majority of the others, the swans,

Canada geese, and ducks preferred the Mattamuskeet and Swanquarter Refuges on the mainland, which between them held half a million waterfowl at this time of year.

A few peregrines winter on the Outer Banks, and Varda, having flown a hundred miles and seeing so much life beneath her, decided to come down. The beach was empty enough to suit her and a haze was building up to the south; the weather was about to change, but suddenly, now that she had reached this point of demarcation, there seemed to be a different feeling in the air. She was no longer moving away from winter; she had come to the place where it was held at bay. The great gathering of birds showed it, and if freakish cold storms came up from the south they would disturb the country for a little time only, and move on. A mile south of Oregon Inlet she half closed her wings and dropped her feet; with her wingtips out straight behind her she swung a wide, descending half circle and came rocking down to land on the crest of the beach.

The green combers curled and thundered on the sand; gulls and terns moved crying to and fro, and fish crows went noisily about their affairs. Varda sat in the sunshine, quiet and content in the damp, cool air, watching the life along the beach and over the distant Sound. As the afternoon wore on the haze increased; the horizon drew in, and pale strings of fog crept in from the sea. Varda, knowing that she would have to feed before it thickened and blotted out the world, rose from the sand. She went down the beach like an arrow, not over a foot in the air, and surprising a flock of sandpipers struck down two of them. After she had eaten them she jumped up again and turned back north; a half-buried ship's timber spiked with a row of rusty nails appeared before her and she decided to land upon it. She landed a little too fast, and clumsily; one of her jesses whipped forward. The slit, cut by the falconer to enable him to draw the jess through one eye of the double-eyed swivel and fold it over the other, landed on a nail point. It hung there for a moment; as she took a half step backward to right herself the point of the nail went through the slit and the jess slipped down over the nail.

Fortune, which had brought her safely through so many perils, now turned her other face. The falconer, the man who had watched her on her first day away from the eyrie on the Barrens beneath the Inukok, who had caught her and trained her and put the leather on her, had brought her down. She was fast to the nail, but she didn't know it yet.

She shook herself to straighten her feathers and settled for the night. The fog thickened; the spectral light of the sinking sun faded out, and the wind picked up along the beach. Later it began to rain, and Varda tightened her feathers to sit it out.

THE SEA ISLANDS

THE STORM whipped the Banks most of the night. The meeting currents of the ocean, driven by the wailing wind, clawed at one another and roared in turbulent fury; rain rattled like shot against the towers of the three lighthouses. It was on such a night that the dreams of people were dimly troubled by the legends they had heard or the history that they knew: Blackbeard the pirate on Ocracoke, the vanished colony — the first English settlement in America — on nearby Roanoke Island, the flaming torpedoed vessels of a bygone war, and drowned sailors washing ashore from Diamond Shoals, that graveyard of ships, with its submerged and shifting dunes.

Before dawn the storm had blown itself out, but the waves were still high; there was much white water on the sea and in the inlets. Varda awoke as the high, thin overcast took on its first color, and watched the light strengthen over the smoking sea. She was very wet, having taken the full brunt of the storm, and almost disappeared in a mantle of fine spray when she shook herself. She opened her wings for the breeze to dry and pulled each of her tail feathers through her beak to dress it. Geese and swans began to move about over the Sound; gulls and terns started their endless patrolling between her and the surf, quick little seaside sparrows appeared and flitted about, and sandpipers ran back and forth in the spindrift. A lone piping plover, blown north of its usual winter range, gave its plaintive whistle as it went over her; she cocked her head to follow its flight. She was growing hungry, but she waited a while longer until she was nearly dry and then jumped off the timber.

The jess that had dropped over the nail pulled her up with a jerk and for a moment she hung over the edge of the timber, beating her wings. In the few days of her freedom she had already forgotten the short compass of her captivity and quickly reacted as though an enemy had hold of her; she rolled over, hissing, and struck back. A wild bird would have continued to fight and try to escape until it had broken its primaries on the timber and exhausted itself, but Varda soon saw that there was no enemy; her long experience with the falconer came back. She knew that she was tied again, and scrambled back onto the timber.

She shook herself and settled down to wait until the man came to take her up and let her fly again.

Toward noon a Jeep with two men in it came up the road from the Refuge Headquarters several miles to the south. The driver was a Fish & Wildlife Service man, the other was a nature photographer. He had been taking pictures of ducks from a blind at Mattamuskeet, and thinking that an unusual bird or two might have been blown in by the storm had driven over early that morning. Both men were scanning the sand, but it was the driver who first noticed the shape on the old timber ahead of them and to the right. He stopped the Jeep and brought up the binoculars hanging around his neck.

"Do you have a good shot of a duck hawk?" he asked, after he had looked for a moment.

"Not a good one," the photographer replied. "Have you got something?"

"There's one over there, in juvenile plumage. Damned handsome, too." He slid the neck strap over his head, handed his companion the glasses, and pointed out Varda on her timber.

The photographer looked at her. "Handsome she is," he said. "Do you think we can get closer?"

"We can try. They don't mind cars much." He ran up the road far enough to get the sun behind them and turning off onto the sand headed for the falcon. Varda sat quietly and watched them.

"She's certainly tame enough," the photographer said. "Maybe we could get closer yet."

They drove closer, and Varda still sat quietly.

"Beautiful," the photographer said, as he took his pictures. "That golden color . . ."

"Got enough?"

"Wait a minute. I'll step out and get a shot as she takes off." He opened the door and stepped out of the Jeep.

He was wearing the same sort of windbreaker that the falconer had frequently worn, and when he stepped out Varda recognized it. She had been sitting all night and all morning, and wanted to fly; she faced him as she had often faced the falconer in similar circumstances, and opened her wings. The photographer was looking through his view-finder, and saw this. It seemed rather odd to him, but he snapped his picture, dropped the camera to the end of its strap which he was holding in his left hand, and turned his head. "What do you make of that?" he asked. "She looks as though she wanted to fly at me, instead of scramming off."

When the camera dropped it looked like a lure to Varda; being quite hungry by this time she forgot that she didn't have the length of the leash to move in, and jumped toward it. The jess pulled her up; she hung for a moment and scrambled back onto the timber, her bells ringing.

The men ran to the falcon, which sat and watched them come, and then they saw the tackle on her and the jess caught on the nail.

"I'll be damned," said the man from the Refuge. "A falconer's bird." He sqatted down, freed the jess, and took the ends of both jesses in his gloved fingers; Varda stepped up onto his fist, shook herself, and sat quietly looking at them, responding again to the habit she had lived under for so long.

"Let's get this stuff off her," the photographer said after a moment. "You do it while I hold her."

"You're going to let her go?"

"Sure. Wouldn't you, after a break like this? We almost went off and left her, and there are ten million other places she could have hung up forever, where no one would ever have found her. The bells first, I guess."

Neither of them was familiar with hawk tackle, and found it insoluble; they ended by cutting it off with a pocket knife. Cast into the air, Varda went off in a wide circle to return high above them and hang head to the wind. They watched her for a long moment, and as they walked back to the Jeep the man from the Refuge looked at the bells and saw the falconer's name and address on them.

"I'll write the guy and tell him what happened," he

said. "I hope the next bird that gets away from him is as lucky."

After the men had disappeared into the Jeep and driven away Varda turned down the beach. Her last connection with men had gone; the bells which had signaled her every move and to which she had become accustomed were off her now, and it would be a little while until she grew used to the silence. She gained height and swung over the marshes on the Sound side; before she reached Refuge Headquarters she took a clapper rail that had been flushed from the marsh by a hunting cat and fed upon it.

When she had finished she sat for a little while in indecision, for there were conflicting inclinations in her. One was to stay for a while where she was, on the Banks, where there was plenty of prey, but it was the weakest one; she remembered too well being fast to the ship's timber. Another was to wander off to the west, to the mainland that she had seen from the air. This would take her over another Refuge, the big lake at Mattamuskeet which was surrounded by canals that had once been dug in a scheme to drain the lake. The canals were beyond the Refuge boundaries and spotted with blinds where guns were always busy. It would have been a dangerous neighborhood for her, but she didn't know that.

The third inclination, the one that had started her away from the Barrens and was still strong, was for the south. It was pleasant enough now where she was; the weather wasn't pushing her yet; it had been unusually good during her passage, but an intuition told her that it could still worsen and bring fogs, cold, and riotous storms to lash the Outer Banks. As she sat among the plucked feathers of the rail this intuition and the dim urge for a place passed down through the germ plasm by the tiercel her father resolved her indecision. She jumped into the air and turned to the south.

Now that the decision was made she loitered no longer; her wings sang on the air as she took a fast and purposeful pace, a few feet above the water, angling down across the Sound. Ducks in the air took to the water or avoided as quickly as they were able the path of her swift and formidable shape. She rose to cross Okracoke, its harbor encircled by live oaks, green yaupon holly glowing with berries, and gaillardia still blooming in the fields.

She crossed land again west of Morehead City; a Marine Corps fighter pilot from Cherry Point Air Station, coming in from a practice flight over the sea, saw her make a playful vertical stoop at a soaring redtail hawk and bound up again several feet above it, and acknowledged to himself that there were times when he and his expensive and complicated equipment seemed inadequate. By the time he was telling of it, with gestures, in the bar of the Officers' Club, Varda was forty miles down the coast and still flying strongly. She had already forgotten the redtail, which had been her only diversion for the afternoon.

Behind the string of pale, sandy barrier beaches that she

passed, between it and the mainland's covering of pines, the country was slowly changing its face. The low, flat marshes widened into broad grassy savannas and swamps of dark water filled with cypresses and cedars and winter-bare gum, tupelo, and cottonwood trees draped with Spanish moss; sweet bay, dwarf honeysuckle and Carolina jessamine, outriders from among the plants that avoided winter, were moving in. Venus's-flytrap, that carnivorous plant that grows only in the Carolinas, lived in the bogs.

As the sun dipped low Varda came down, tired and hungry, in a long slanting stoop back over the marsh to take a black-crowned night heron coming out to feed. He stabbed at her eyes as she closed him at speed, but she rolled sideways, caught him with her outthrust feet by the head and the middle of the back, and carried him to a little offshore island to feed upon.

The sky's powdering of stars brightened as the light faded from the sky, and on the Inland Waterway between her and the shoreside marshes a yacht moved south; very faintly, music came to her over the darkening water.

Before the rim of the sun had come over the horizon to lay its golden light on the sea Varda had fed and was in the air. Her course was a little south of southwest, twenty miles off the coast; the wind lay behind her, not too strong for comfort, and helped her along. Presently she was past the North Carolina line, into a subtropical world, where the barrier islands ended for a time and a wide, unbroken beach, backed by myrtle and palmetto, ran for fifty miles. She flew low over the water, too low to see several sperm whales as they rose from the depths to blow two miles west of her, passing a little Audubon's shearwater which seemed lost and alone as it flew northward with rapid wingbeats over the empty sea.

She made her landfall over the tip of North Island, where the Santee empties into Winyah Bay and the Atlantic, and the barrier islands begin again with the sea islands behind them. She was on the edge of the Low Country, where the flat sea islands are separated by wide salt marshes and slow tidal rivers and creeks winding inland with great swamps about them; rice-growing country in the bygone days when it was possible with slave labor to do the endless diking and ditching and planting, and uncounted legions of bobolinks, "reed birds," fed and sang their rollicking songs in the autumn and spring as they migrated to South America and back. Shot by the million for years up and down the coast and sold in the markets in bunches, they were much reduced now, and rice was no longer grown; the dikes had fallen to ruin, and tourists came in the spring to a few of the lovely great old plantation houses to see their gardens of camellias and azalea, bamboo, live oaks, and tropical flowers.

There had been no bays for waterfowl behind the long beach that Varda had been passing, but now that the barrier islands had reappeared, with wide marshes and the Inland

Waterway behind them, there was a profusion of them. She had come to one of the greatest wintering grounds along the Atlantic coast for shore birds, those travelers whose rueful voices hold all of the wide and empty desolation of the far north. The afternoon was waning as she came in sight of Cape Romain Refuge and the wide marshes again. She flew on over the Bay toward Bull Island, unspoiled jewel among the sea islands; offshore from the ocean beach a few brown pelicans flew solemnly along, seeming in their outlandish configuration to have come out of the prehistoric world, and on the long sandspit edging the Bay a great congregation was feeding because the tide was out. There were sandpipers, dowitchers, black-bellied plover, long-billed curlews and oyster catchers which found open oysters and clipped the closing muscle with their specialized bills to prevent the oyster from shutting up his armored house against them.

Varda saw them from a distance on the sandspit, against the background of gaunt gray trees that the encroaching ocean had killed. She had flown two hundred miles since dawn and was tired and very hungry; with all this prey before her she had only to make her choice. She built up her speed and came in low and fast like a fighter pilot making a ground-strafing run; there was a frenzied flutter of wings before her, and in the wild confusion she struck a big black-bellied plover just as it took alarm and jumped twisting into the air. Quiet gradually returned as she plucked it, and a wide, empty circle was left around her; the birds ignored her, now that she was feeding and no longer a threat to their lives. The tide began to come in as Varda finished, and she decided to spend the night in a tree.

She got up and flew toward the forest, over the fresh-water ponds full of wintering ducks, found a high dead pine beside a creek in the swamp, and landed on a limb near the top. A pileated woodpecker had been climbing about on the other side of it, and dropped for cover with a loud startled cry and a spectacular flash of black and white and the red of his crest.

The thick subtropical forest of laurel oaks, live oaks, magnolias and loblolly pines, looped with heavy creeping vines and draped with long veils of Spanish moss, stretched all around Varda; palmetto, wax myrtle and holly, green-briar and red bay covered the ground below. In this en-tangled and exuberant world, so unlike the Barrens, the lives of the creatures which moved about below her were secret and concealed; but she heard a flock of wild turkeys fly up to roost in the distance, their big wings beating against the branches, and farther off a barred owl greeted the coming night with its series of emphatic hoots that had a nasal, snarling end. In the segment of the creek that she could see below her there was sudden movement and rip-ples that slid silently and as smooth as oil; a pair of otters were playing together with a beautiful fluid grace and searching the banks for crawfish.

Varda watched them, craning her neck, until the intervening shrubbery hid them from view. When they were gone she made a low, creaking sound, as though from a sense of loss. She had wanted them to stay; perhaps she felt a sort of kinship with them, for their mastery of their element and their gay and happy hearts.

JOURNEY'S END

During the hours of the night while Varda slept and the raccoons hunted the creek banks, the deer moved softly about on the trails that human visitors walked by day, and the little flying squirrels with their large, dark eyes slid down the air from tree to tree, the impulse that had brought her so far strengthened even more. It had been intermittent, varying in intensity, sometimes a little confused; it had been interfered with by her captivity and weakened for the moment by Hatteras, but when dawn paled the sky it was pulling strongly at her. Darkness still held the tangle beneath her when she left the pine; she flew to the shoreside

marshes and killed and fed, and got into the air again.

She gained height; ducks were moving now, and south on a dead tree along the Inland Waterway a resident bald eagle sat quietly with the early light gleaming on his white head. She swung seaward, across the long, broad beach, high above the pelicans and scoters beyond the surf, and picked up her wingbeat for a long day's reach. At times she would be twenty-five miles or more off the coast, and see little but the marching waves; the day would wear out most of its long and lonely hours over the sea. She passed close enough to Charleston to see the city well, the walls of Fort Sumter in the harbor and further west the spidery steelwork of the harbor bridge, and then the coast line began to fall away from her course. She passed far seaward of Beaufort and its white, columned houses where inland rice plantation owners had once come in summer to be cooler near the ocean, and Savannah where Sherman ended his grievous march to the sea; passing seaward of the entire coast of Georgia she made her landfall near St. Marys Entrance north of Jacksonville.

The vicinity didn't suit her, but being hungry she picked a boat-tailed grackle out of the air above the coastal marsh. It wasn't large enough to replace the energy she had used up in the day's flying; but it satisfied her for the moment, and on an impulse she took to the air again and swung west. The sun was well down the sky now, but within the hour she was over the marshes on the southeastern end of Okefenokee Swamp and took a wood duck as it arose from

among the water lilies and spatterdocks filling a little creek.
She was plucking it in the middle of a sandy clearing on a
nearby island when a possum, wandering on its slow way
through the underbrush with its tail curled around a hand-
ful of dried leaves which it was taking back to its tree hollow for bedding, stopped a few feet away and turned its
pale, pointed face toward her. Varda paused and turned
in its direction. She was unfamiliar with this creature, but
had no intention of giving up the duck; she lowered her
head and stared menacingly at it, and it went on.

By the time Varda finished the duck the sun had dropped
below the horizon; the cloud banks in the western sky
flamed with the colors of sunset, dyeing faintly the islands
of winter-brown cypress, gum, and tupelo trees with their
long, ghostly pendants of Spanish moss and the low vegeta-
tion of the marsh. Varda flew high into a tall cypress for
the night. On another island not far away a barred owl
began its hooting, to be drowned out by a chorus of hair-
raising wails by the limpkins of the marsh. Presently they
all ceased their clamor and silence fell again; Varda settled
herself. All around her the vast drowned land, untouched
and primitive, trackless, broken by islands choked with
climbing vines and impenetrable underbrush and covered
by great moss-draped trees, had not changed since the time
when the Spanish explorer De Soto was so baffled by its
labyrinths that he had to turn away. Now darkness and
eerie silence fell upon its brown, vegetation-filled waters
wandering south toward St. Marys River; the night crea-

tures began to move about, a distant alligator bellowed once, and Varda slept.

Varda was awakened by the hysterical scolding of two parula warblers, which had found a cottonmouth moccasin lying torpidly across several branches in the underbrush below her, and were scolding it; she shook herself and prepared for the day. A small flight of egrets went over her head, their white feathers dyed faintly by the rising sun. She watched a flock of sandhill cranes scale down over an island in the distance, landing with great wing flappings in the marsh, and dropped from her high perch in the cypress. There was a great deal of open prairie in the part of the Okefenokee in which she had spent the night, but she wanted to get above it and gained height at once.

She turned south. Soon she was past the Florida line, and continued on her way down the low, rolling backbone of the state. Pineland, prairie and scrubland fell behind her, and dense thickets of scrub palmetto and myrtle. She saw a Cooper's hawk burst out of one of these thickets after a scrub jay; but the jay managed to dive into other cover and the hawk pitched up to land on one wire of an electric line. As it teetered to balance itself its long tail touched another wire. There was a brilliant flash of blue fire and the hawk, its feet clenched by the galvanic shock, dropped head down and hung dead.

Varda was startled by the lethal flash, swung away from it and went on. There were more pinelands now and the underbrush grew scantier under the pines. The birds which lived in it were mostly redcockaded woodpeckers, nuthatches, and pine warblers, fitter prey for Cooper's and sharp-shinned hawks. But the lakes and streams, bordered by cypress and hardwoods, presently began to increase; these waters and the swamps around them were full of ducks, herons, and marsh birds and were more to her style of hunting. As she came over one of the little lakes a small flock of blue-winged teal rounded a point and didn't see her at first. She rolled over, folded her wings, and went straight down.

The teal scattered, most of them dropping for the water; but one drake, his white face patch gleaming, wheeled off for the woods and put on speed. Varda had marked him; she shifted the direction of her stoop and flashed after him. He was very fast, and shifty; the swift chase circled through the cypresses and Spanish moss back toward the lake again. The drake saw open water ahead of him through the trees and dropped toward it. Varda had pulled up on him; she rolled over onto her back, slid beneath him and the water, and picked him up. She was so close to the ground that the waterside grasses brushed her back. There was a man spinfishing in a rowboat offshore, and he stared with open mouth as Varda rocketed past his head carrying the drake; he watched her until she went through the trees across the lake and dropped from sight.

She came down in an opening, broke the drake's neck, and gave the sharp, hoarse peregrine croak before she began to plume her quarry. The wild intricate chase through the trees and its successful conclusion had greatly pleased her. There was a tawny movement off in the underbrush and she turned toward it. A bobcat had been moving past the opening, back in the underbrush; it had seen her come down, and began to stalk her.

Varda watched it, for it was a creature large enough to be very dangerous. The cat, belly to the ground and eyes fixed on her, moved to a spot where there was a clear path through the underbrush; Varda jumped into the air as it launched itself toward her. The bobcat arose on its hind legs, missed her with a big paw, and turned to the teal.

Varda mounted up through the trees, higher and higher. She was filled with wrath at the thieving cat; swinging behind it, she rolled over and stooped, beating her wings rapidly to build up speed. The bobcat was standing head-down sniffing the teal, and she went up the middle of its back with beautiful precision, drawing a thin, bloody line on its hide with a rear talon. The cat reared, snarling, and swung at her, but she was past it and high in the air again; she hung there for a moment and stooped again as soon as its head was turned, flitting like a phantom through the trees, twisting, bounding up, lost in the Spanish moss one instant and suddenly reappearing from another quarter the next. The bobcat whirled and spat and swung its big hooked paws at her; it was a deadly game, and few peregrines would have chanced it, but Varda's blood was up. When the cat had moved far enough from the teal Varda swooped, picked it off the ground without slackening her pace, and bore it off to another opening a mile away.

Varda found the long vistas of opening grasslands and swamps near Lake Kissimmee to her taste as she went through that country. She circled for a moment and watched as an Audubon's caracara, that awkward-appearing and aggressive hawk, quarreled with the turkey vultures around the carcass of a steer, was unaware of the odd little burrowing owls that loved that place, and saw many sandhill cranes.

She slept that night near Lake Istokpoga, and crossed Observation Island in Lake Okeechobee the next morning. There were several Everglades kites among the gathering of herons, egrets, and ibises, flying low over the great swamp, hunting for the snails that were the kites' only food; man's extensive draining of the swamps where the snail lived had brought it and the dark bird that fed upon it to the edge of extinction.

Varda went on, through the Everglades. That vast and watery world of sawgrass, ponds, and hammocks of great moss-draped trees, so often thought of as a world of trackless desolation, was full of life: great white herons, ibises, egrets, anhingas, and gaudy gallinules. Here the plume hunters had killed them in bygone days, leaving countless nestlings to starve or feed the fishes or the fish crows; now they were protected. This swarming life, wading and soaring in the warm air, feeding and quarreling and almost ready to mate and raise their broods once more, brought constant color and movement to the Everglades world. There were too many of them for Varda, and she didn't like their grassy world; she took a higher pitch and saw the mangroves begin and the waters of Florida Bay.

She went on, higher still above the shoreside tangle, the marshes of the Bay and the waterways through them, the mangrove islands and ungainly pelicans and herons in the twisting branches, a big shark or two working the flats; but very soon she saw the ocean and its lovely colors and the scattered islands of the Keys.

The Atlantic side of the Keys was where she wanted to go; the wide purple water, shading to blue and emerald and aquamarine clear as air in the afternoon sun, drew her like a magnet. She crossed high over Islamorada and the cars on the highway, and a few miles south of the town, sur-rounded by the sea, there was a lonely island with neither road nor house nor sign of man on it, and a gleaming crescent of sandy beach. She saw it with something like a shock of recognition, although her own eyes had never seen it before; drawing in her wings she slid down the air in a wide, descending half circle to land on the beach.

There was a scattering of flat-bottomed cumulus clouds out over the sea; behind her the island rose a little and was thick as a tropical jungle with coconut palms, gumbo-limbo, silver palms, wild tamarinds and a dense tangle of mangroves and climbing vines.

Varda looked all about and then shook herself; then she

made her low, creaking sound. The urge to move farther south had gone; already she felt at home. She would wander about a little because it was her nature, but unless she was too much disturbed she would return to the island from her wanderings until the restlessness of spring washed over her and started her to the far Barrens again.

Her cere and legs and feet, which had been pale cerulean when she left the eyrie, were yellow now, and there were a few of the slaty blue feathers of maturity among the dark brown feathers on her back. She would not molt all at once and be flightless for a time like the ducks and geese; little by little her golden color would change. By Easter, with good fortune, she would be a thousand miles or more up the coast. It would not be very long now, for she had come late.

The blossoms of spring would go with her, the northern world would flower again, and bumblebees would be among the tiny bushes hugging the warming sweep of the tundra. She would be one of a tremendous tide of fragile winged creatures: northern phalaropes from the coast of Peru, Arctic terns from the edge of the Antarctic ice, parasitic jaegers from New Zealand, small wheatears from Africa across the north Atlantic, and uncountable legions of others from the lands of the winter sun.

This going would be a wondrous thing, a great march across the limitless and stormy pathways of the sky, a miracle.